Postal

Exam Secrets Study Guide

DEAR FUTURE EXAM SUCCESS STORY

First of all, **THANK YOU** for purchasing Mometrix study materials!

Second, congratulations! You are one of the few determined test-takers who are committed to doing whatever it takes to excel on your exam. **You have come to the right place.** We developed these study materials with one goal in mind: to deliver you the information you need in a format that's concise and easy to use.

In addition to optimizing your guide for the content of the test, we've outlined our recommended steps for breaking down the preparation process into small, attainable goals so you can make sure you stay on track.

We've also analyzed the entire test-taking process, identifying the most common pitfalls and showing how you can overcome them and be ready for any curveball the test throws you.

Standardized testing is one of the biggest obstacles on your road to success, which only increases the importance of doing well in the high-pressure, high-stakes environment of test day. Your results on this test could have a significant impact on your future, and this guide provides the information and practical advice to help you achieve your full potential on test day.

Your success is our success

We would love to hear from you! If you would like to share the story of your exam success or if you have any questions or comments in regard to our products, please contact us at **800-673-8175** or **support@mometrix.com**.

Thanks again for your business and we wish you continued success!

Sincerely,
The Mometrix Test Preparation Team

Written and edited by the Mometrix Exam Secrets Test Prep Team
Printed in the United States of America

TABLE OF CONTENTS

INTRODUCTION 1
SECRET KEY 1: PLAN BIG, STUDY SMALL 2
SECRET KEY 2: MAKE YOUR STUDYING COUNT 4
SECRET KEY 3: PRACTICE THE RIGHT WAY 6
SECRET KEY 4: PACE YOURSELF 8
SECRET KEY 5: HAVE A PLAN FOR GUESSING 9
TEST-TAKING STRATEGIES 12
VIRTUAL ENTRY ASSESSMENT (VEA) 17
- OVERVIEW 17
- VEAS & SECTIONS 17
- WORK SCENARIOS 18
- TELL US YOUR STORY 21
- DESCRIBE YOUR APPROACH 23
- CHECK FOR ERRORS 26
- WORK YOUR REGISTER 28

POSTAL EXAM PRACTICE TEST 33
- WORK SCENARIOS 33
- TELL US YOUR STORY 37
- DESCRIBE YOUR APPROACH 38
- CHECK FOR ERRORS 42
- WORK YOUR REGISTER 58

ANSWER KEY AND EXPLANATIONS 91
- WORK SCENARIOS 91
- DESCRIBE YOUR APPROACH 93
- CHECK FOR ERRORS 99
- WORK YOUR REGISTER 107

HOW TO OVERCOME TEST ANXIETY 131
ADDITIONAL BONUS MATERIAL 138

Introduction

Thank you for purchasing this resource! You have made the choice to prepare yourself for a test that could have a huge impact on your future, and this guide is designed to help you be fully ready for test day. Obviously, it's important to have a solid understanding of the test material, but you also need to be prepared for the unique environment and stressors of the test, so that you can perform to the best of your abilities.

For this purpose, the first section that appears in this guide is the **Secret Keys**. We've devoted countless hours to meticulously researching what works and what doesn't, and we've boiled down our findings to the five most impactful steps you can take to improve your performance on the test. We start at the beginning with study planning and move through the preparation process, all the way to the testing strategies that will help you get the most out of what you know when you're finally sitting in front of the test.

We recommend that you start preparing for your test as far in advance as possible. However, if you've bought this guide as a last-minute study resource and only have a few days before your test, we recommend that you skip over the first two Secret Keys since they address a long-term study plan.

If you struggle with **test anxiety**, we strongly encourage you to check out our recommendations for how you can overcome it. Test anxiety is a formidable foe, but it can be beaten, and we want to make sure you have the tools you need to defeat it.

Secret Key 1: Plan Big, Study Small

There's a lot riding on your performance. If you want to ace this test, you're going to need to keep your skills sharp and the material fresh in your mind. You need a plan that lets you review everything you need to know while still fitting in your schedule. We'll break this strategy down into three categories.

Information Organization

Start with the information you already have: the official test outline. From this, you can make a complete list of all the concepts you need to cover before the test. Organize these concepts into groups that can be studied together, and create a list of any related vocabulary you need to learn so you can brush up on any difficult terms. You'll want to keep this vocabulary list handy once you actually start studying since you may need to add to it along the way.

Time Management

Once you have your set of study concepts, decide how to spread them out over the time you have left before the test. Break your study plan into small, clear goals so you have a manageable task for each day and know exactly what you're doing. Then just focus on one small step at a time. When you manage your time this way, you don't need to spend hours at a time studying. Studying a small block of content for a short period each day helps you retain information better and avoid stressing over how much you have left to do. You can relax knowing that you have a plan to cover everything in time. In order for this strategy to be effective though, you have to start studying early and stick to your schedule. Avoid the exhaustion and futility that comes from last-minute cramming!

Study Environment

The environment you study in has a big impact on your learning. Studying in a coffee shop, while probably more enjoyable, is not likely to be as fruitful as studying in a quiet room. It's important to keep distractions to a minimum. You're only planning to study for a short block of time, so make the most of it. Don't pause to check your phone or get up to find a snack. It's also important to **avoid multitasking**. Research has consistently shown that multitasking will make your studying dramatically less effective. Your study area should also be comfortable and well-lit so you don't have the distraction of straining your eyes or sitting on an uncomfortable chair.

The time of day you study is also important. You want to be rested and alert. Don't wait until just before bedtime. Study when you'll be most likely to comprehend and remember. Even better, if you know what time of day your test will be, set that time aside for study. That way your brain will be used to working on that subject at that specific time and you'll have a better chance of recalling information.

Finally, it can be helpful to team up with others who are studying for the same test. Your actual studying should be done in as isolated an environment as possible, but the work of organizing the information and setting up the study plan can be divided up. In between study sessions, you can discuss with your teammates the concepts that you're all studying and quiz each other on the details. Just be sure that your teammates are as serious about the test as you are. If you find that your study time is being replaced with social time, you might need to find a new team.

Secret Key 2: Make Your Studying Count

You're devoting a lot of time and effort to preparing for this test, so you want to be absolutely certain it will pay off. This means doing more than just reading the content and hoping you can remember it on test day. It's important to make every minute of study count. There are two main areas you can focus on to make your studying count.

Retention

It doesn't matter how much time you study if you can't remember the material. You need to make sure you are retaining the concepts. To check your retention of the information you're learning, try recalling it at later times with minimal prompting. Try carrying around flashcards and glance at one or two from time to time or ask a friend who's also studying for the test to quiz you.

To enhance your retention, look for ways to put the information into practice so that you can apply it rather than simply recalling it. If you're using the information in practical ways, it will be much easier to remember. Similarly, it helps to solidify a concept in your mind if you're not only reading it to yourself but also explaining it to someone else. Ask a friend to let you teach them about a concept you're a little shaky on (or speak aloud to an imaginary audience if necessary). As you try to summarize, define, give examples, and answer your friend's questions, you'll understand the concepts better and they will stay with you longer. Finally, step back for a big picture view and ask yourself how each piece of information fits with the whole subject. When you link the different concepts together and see them working together as a whole, it's easier to remember the individual components.

Finally, practice showing your work on any multi-step problems, even if you're just studying. Writing out each step you take to solve a problem will help solidify the process in your mind, and you'll be more likely to remember it during the test.

Modality

Modality simply refers to the means or method by which you study. Choosing a study modality that fits your own individual learning style is crucial. No two people learn best in exactly the same way, so it's important to know your strengths and use them to your advantage.

For example, if you learn best by visualization, focus on visualizing a concept in your mind and draw an image or a diagram. Try color-coding your notes, illustrating them, or creating symbols that will trigger your mind to recall a learned concept. If you learn best by hearing or discussing information, find a study partner who learns the same way or read aloud to yourself. Think about how to put the information in your own words. Imagine that you are giving a lecture on the topic and record yourself so you can listen to it later.

For any learning style, flashcards can be helpful. Organize the information so you can take advantage of spare moments to review. Underline key words or phrases. Use different colors for different categories. Mnemonic devices (such as creating a short list in which every item starts with the same letter) can also help with retention. Find what works best for you and use it to store the information in your mind most effectively and easily.

Secret Key 3: Practice the Right Way

Your success on test day depends not only on how many hours you put into preparing, but also on whether you prepared the right way. It's good to check along the way to see if your studying is paying off. One of the most effective ways to do this is by taking practice tests to evaluate your progress. Practice tests are useful because they show exactly where you need to improve. Every time you take a practice test, pay special attention to these three groups of questions:

- The questions you got wrong
- The questions you had to guess on, even if you guessed right
- The questions you found difficult or slow to work through

This will show you exactly what your weak areas are, and where you need to devote more study time. Ask yourself why each of these questions gave you trouble. Was it because you didn't understand the material? Was it because you didn't remember the vocabulary? Do you need more repetitions on this type of question to build speed and confidence? Dig into those questions and figure out how you can strengthen your weak areas as you go back to review the material.

Additionally, many practice tests have a section explaining the answer choices. It can be tempting to read the explanation and think that you now have a good understanding of the concept. However, an explanation likely only covers part of the question's broader context. Even if the explanation makes perfect sense, **go back and investigate** every concept related to the question until you're positive you have a thorough understanding.

As you go along, keep in mind that the practice test is just that: practice. Memorizing these questions and answers will not be very helpful on the actual test because it is unlikely to have any of the same exact questions. If you only know the right answers to the sample questions, you won't be prepared for the real thing. **Study the concepts** until you understand them fully, and then you'll be able to answer any question that shows up on the test.

It's important to wait on the practice tests until you're ready. If you take a test on your first day of study, you may be overwhelmed by the amount of material covered and how much you need to learn. Work up to it gradually.

On test day, you'll need to be prepared for answering questions, managing your time, and using the test-taking strategies you've learned. It's a lot to balance, like a mental marathon that will have a big impact on your future. Like training for a marathon, you'll need to start slowly and work your way up. When test day arrives, you'll be ready.

Start with the strategies you've read in the first two Secret Keys—plan your course and study in the way that works best for you. If you have time, consider using multiple study resources to get different approaches to the same concepts. It can be helpful to see difficult concepts from more than one angle. Then find a good source for practice tests. Many times, the test website will suggest potential study resources or provide sample tests.

Practice Test Strategy

If you're able to find at least three practice tests, we recommend this strategy:

Untimed and Open-Book Practice

Take the first test with no time constraints and with your notes and study guide handy. Take your time and focus on applying the strategies you've learned.

Timed and Open-Book Practice

Take the second practice test open-book as well, but set a timer and practice pacing yourself to finish in time.

Timed and Closed-Book Practice

Take any other practice tests as if it were test day. Set a timer and put away your study materials. Sit at a table or desk in a quiet room, imagine yourself at the testing center, and answer questions as quickly and accurately as possible.

Keep repeating timed and closed-book tests on a regular basis until you run out of practice tests or it's time for the actual test. Your mind will be ready for the schedule and stress of test day, and you'll be able to focus on recalling the material you've learned.

Secret Key 4: Pace Yourself

Once you're fully prepared for the material on the test, your biggest challenge on test day will be managing your time. Just knowing that the clock is ticking can make you panic even if you have plenty of time left. Work on pacing yourself so you can build confidence against the time constraints of the exam. Pacing is a difficult skill to master, especially in a high-pressure environment, so **practice is vital.**

Set time expectations for your pace based on how much time is available. For example, if a section has 60 questions and the time limit is 30 minutes, you know you have to average 30 seconds or less per question in order to answer them all. Although 30 seconds is the hard limit, set 25 seconds per question as your goal, so you reserve extra time to spend on harder questions. When you budget extra time for the harder questions, you no longer have any reason to stress when those questions take longer to answer.

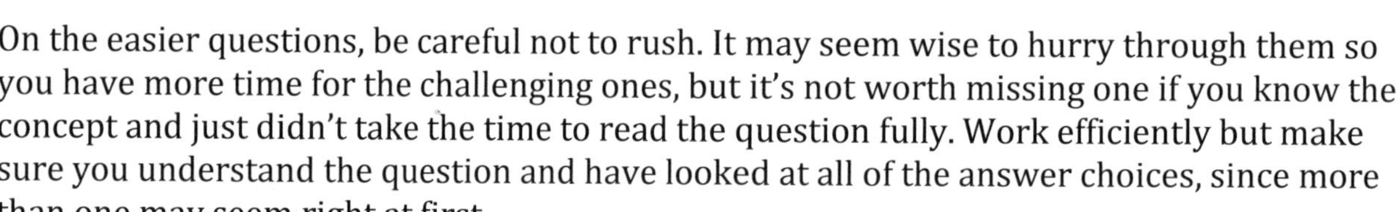

Don't let this time expectation distract you from working through the test at a calm, steady pace, but keep it in mind so you don't spend too much time on any one question. Recognize that taking extra time on one question you don't understand may keep you from answering two that you do understand later in the test. If your time limit for a question is up and you're still not sure of the answer, mark it and move on, and come back to it later if the time and the test format allow. If the testing format doesn't allow you to return to earlier questions, just make an educated guess; then put it out of your mind and move on.

On the easier questions, be careful not to rush. It may seem wise to hurry through them so you have more time for the challenging ones, but it's not worth missing one if you know the concept and just didn't take the time to read the question fully. Work efficiently but make sure you understand the question and have looked at all of the answer choices, since more than one may seem right at first.

Even if you're paying attention to the time, you may find yourself a little behind at some point. You should speed up to get back on track, but do so wisely. Don't panic; just take a few seconds less on each question until you're caught up. Don't guess without thinking, but do look through the answer choices and eliminate any you know are wrong. If you can get down to two choices, it is often worthwhile to guess from those. Once you've chosen an answer, move on and don't dwell on any that you skipped or had to hurry through. If a question was taking too long, chances are it was one of the harder ones, so you weren't as likely to get it right anyway.

On the other hand, if you find yourself getting ahead of schedule, it may be beneficial to slow down a little. The more quickly you work, the more likely you are to make a careless mistake that will affect your score. You've budgeted time for each question, so don't be afraid to spend that time. Practice an efficient but careful pace to get the most out of the time you have.

Secret Key 5: Have a Plan for Guessing

When you're taking the test, you may find yourself stuck on a question. Some of the answer choices seem better than others, but you don't see the one answer choice that is obviously correct. What do you do?

The scenario described above is very common, yet most test takers have not effectively prepared for it. Developing and practicing a plan for guessing may be one of the single most effective uses of your time as you get ready for the exam.

In developing your plan for guessing, there are three questions to address:

- When should you start the guessing process?
- How should you narrow down the choices?
- Which answer should you choose?

When to Start the Guessing Process

Unless your plan for guessing is to select C every time (which, despite its merits, is not what we recommend), you need to leave yourself enough time to apply your answer elimination strategies. Since you have a limited amount of time for each question, that means that if you're going to give yourself the best shot at guessing correctly, you have to decide quickly whether or not you will guess.

Of course, the best-case scenario is that you don't have to guess at all, so first, see if you can answer the question based on your knowledge of the subject and basic reasoning skills. Focus on the key words in the question and try to jog your memory of related topics. Give yourself a chance to bring the knowledge to mind, but once you realize that you don't have (or you can't access) the knowledge you need to answer the question, it's time to start the guessing process.

It's almost always better to start the guessing process too early than too late. It only takes a few seconds to remember something and answer the question from knowledge. Carefully eliminating wrong answer choices takes longer. Plus, going through the process of eliminating answer choices can actually help jog your memory.

Summary: Start the guessing process as soon as you decide that you can't answer the question based on your knowledge.

How to Narrow Down the Choices

The next chapter in this book (**Test-Taking Strategies**) includes a wide range of strategies for how to approach questions and how to look for answer choices to eliminate. You will definitely want to read those carefully, practice them, and figure out which ones work best for you. Here though, we're going to address a mindset rather than a particular strategy.

Your odds of guessing an answer correctly depend on how many options you are choosing from.

Number of options left	5	4	3	2	1
Odds of guessing correctly	20%	25%	33%	50%	100%

You can see from this chart just how valuable it is to be able to eliminate incorrect answers and make an educated guess, but there are two things that many test takers do that cause them to miss out on the benefits of guessing:

- Accidentally eliminating the correct answer
- Selecting an answer based on an impression

We'll look at the first one here, and the second one in the next section.

To avoid accidentally eliminating the correct answer, we recommend a thought exercise called **the $5 challenge**. In this challenge, you only eliminate an answer choice from contention if you are willing to bet $5 on it being wrong. Why $5? Five dollars is a small but not insignificant amount of money. It's an amount you could afford to lose but wouldn't want to throw away. And while losing $5 once might not hurt too much, doing it twenty times will set you back $100. In the same way, each small decision you make—eliminating a choice here, guessing on a question there—won't by itself impact your score very much, but when you put them all together, they can make a big difference. By holding each answer choice elimination decision to a higher standard, you can reduce the risk of accidentally eliminating the correct answer.

The $5 challenge can also be applied in a positive sense: If you are willing to bet $5 that an answer choice *is* correct, go ahead and mark it as correct.

Summary: Only eliminate an answer choice if you are willing to bet $5 that it is wrong.

Which Answer to Choose

You're taking the test. You've run into a hard question and decided you'll have to guess. You've eliminated all the answer choices you're willing to bet $5 on. Now you have to pick an answer. Why do we even need to talk about this? Why can't you just pick whichever one you feel like when the time comes?

The answer to these questions is that if you don't come into the test with a plan, you'll rely on your impression to select an answer choice, and if you do that, you risk falling into a trap. The test writers know that everyone who takes their test will be guessing on some of the questions, so they intentionally write wrong answer choices to seem plausible. You still have to pick an answer though, and if the wrong answer choices are designed to look right, how can you ever be sure that you're not falling for their trap? The best solution we've found to this dilemma is to take the decision out of your hands entirely. Here is the process we recommend:

Once you've eliminated any choices that you are confident (willing to bet $5) are wrong, select the first remaining choice as your answer.

Whether you choose to select the first remaining choice, the second, or the last, the important thing is that you use some preselected standard. Using this approach guarantees that you will not be enticed into selecting an answer choice that looks right, because you are not basing your decision on how the answer choices look.

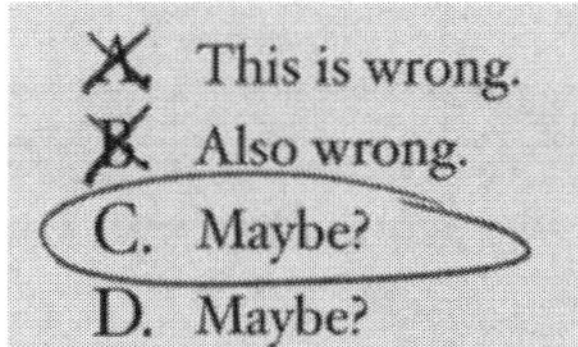

This is not meant to make you question your knowledge. Instead, it is to help you recognize the difference between your knowledge and your impressions. There's a huge difference between thinking an answer is right because of what you know, and thinking an answer is right because it looks or sounds like it should be right.

Summary: To ensure that your selection is appropriately random, make a predetermined selection from among all answer choices you have not eliminated.

Test-Taking Strategies

This section contains a list of test-taking strategies that you may find helpful as you work through the test. By taking what you know and applying logical thought, you can maximize your chances of answering any question correctly!

It is very important to realize that every question is different and every person is different: no single strategy will work on every question, and no single strategy will work for every person. That's why we've included all of them here, so you can try them out and determine which ones work best for different types of questions and which ones work best for you.

Question Strategies

⊘ Read Carefully

Read the question and the answer choices carefully. Don't miss the question because you misread the terms. You have plenty of time to read each question thoroughly and make sure you understand what is being asked. Yet a happy medium must be attained, so don't waste too much time. You must read carefully and efficiently.

⊘ Contextual Clues

Look for contextual clues. If the question includes a word you are not familiar with, look at the immediate context for some indication of what the word might mean. Contextual clues can often give you all the information you need to decipher the meaning of an unfamiliar word. Even if you can't determine the meaning, you may be able to narrow down the possibilities enough to make a solid guess at the answer to the question.

⊘ Prefixes

If you're having trouble with a word in the question or answer choices, try dissecting it. Take advantage of every clue that the word might include. Prefixes can be a huge help. Usually, they allow you to determine a basic meaning. *Pre-* means before, *post-* means after, *pro-* is positive, *de-* is negative. From prefixes, you can get an idea of the general meaning of the word and try to put it into context.

⊘ Hedge Words

Watch out for critical hedge words, such as *likely, may, can, sometimes, often, almost, mostly, usually, generally, rarely,* and *sometimes.* Question writers insert these hedge phrases to cover every possibility. Often an answer choice will be wrong simply because it leaves no room for exception. Be on guard for answer choices that have definitive words such as *exactly* and *always.*

⊘ Switchback Words

Stay alert for *switchbacks*. These are the words and phrases frequently used to alert you to shifts in thought. The most common switchback words are *but*, *although*, and *however*. Others include *nevertheless*, *on the other hand*, *even though*, *while*, *in spite of*, *despite*, and *regardless of*. Switchback words are important to catch because they can change the direction of the question or an answer choice.

⊘ Face Value

When in doubt, use common sense. Accept the situation in the problem at face value. Don't read too much into it. These problems will not require you to make wild assumptions. If you have to go beyond creativity and warp time or space in order to have an answer choice fit the question, then you should move on and consider the other answer choices. These are normal problems rooted in reality. The applicable relationship or explanation may not be readily apparent, but it is there for you to figure out. Use your common sense to interpret anything that isn't clear.

Answer Choice Strategies

⊘ Answer Selection

The most thorough way to pick an answer choice is to identify and eliminate wrong answers until only one is left, then confirm it is the correct answer. Sometimes an answer choice may immediately seem right, but be careful. The test writers will usually put more than one reasonable answer choice on each question, so take a second to read all of them and make sure that the other choices are not equally obvious. As long as you have time left, it is better to read every answer choice than to pick the first one that looks right without checking the others.

⊘ Answer Choice Families

An answer choice family consists of two (in rare cases, three) answer choices that are very similar in construction and cannot all be true at the same time. If you see two answer choices that are direct opposites or parallels, one of them is usually the correct answer. For instance, if one answer choice says that quantity x increases and another either says that quantity x decreases (opposite) or says that quantity y increases (parallel), then those answer choices would fall into the same family. An answer choice that doesn't match the construction of the answer choice family is more likely to be incorrect. Most questions will not have answer choice families, but when they do appear, you should be prepared to recognize them.

⊘ Eliminate Answers

Eliminate answer choices as soon as you realize they are wrong, but make sure you consider all possibilities. If you are eliminating answer choices and realize that the last one you are left with is also wrong, don't panic. Start over and consider each choice again. There may be something you missed the first time that you will realize on the second pass.

✓ Avoid Fact Traps

Don't be distracted by an answer choice that is factually true but doesn't answer the question. You are looking for the choice that answers the question. Stay focused on what the question is asking for so you don't accidentally pick an answer that is true but incorrect. Always go back to the question and make sure the answer choice you've selected actually answers the question and is not merely a true statement.

✓ Extreme Statements

In general, you should avoid answers that put forth extreme actions as standard practice or proclaim controversial ideas as established fact. An answer choice that states the "process should be used in certain situations, if…" is much more likely to be correct than one that states the "process should be discontinued completely." The first is a calm rational statement and doesn't even make a definitive, uncompromising stance, using a hedge word *if* to provide wiggle room, whereas the second choice is far more extreme.

✓ Benchmark

As you read through the answer choices and you come across one that seems to answer the question well, mentally select that answer choice. This is not your final answer, but it's the one that will help you evaluate the other answer choices. The one that you selected is your benchmark or standard for judging each of the other answer choices. Every other answer choice must be compared to your benchmark. That choice is correct until proven otherwise by another answer choice beating it. If you find a better answer, then that one becomes your new benchmark. Once you've decided that no other choice answers the question as well as your benchmark, you have your final answer.

✓ Predict the Answer

Before you even start looking at the answer choices, it is often best to try to predict the answer. When you come up with the answer on your own, it is easier to avoid distractions and traps because you will know exactly what to look for. The right answer choice is unlikely to be word-for-word what you came up with, but it should be a close match. Even if you are confident that you have the right answer, you should still take the time to read each option before moving on.

General Strategies

✓ Tough Questions

If you are stumped on a problem or it appears too hard or too difficult, don't waste time. Move on! Remember though, if you can quickly check for obviously incorrect answer choices, your chances of guessing correctly are greatly improved. Before you completely give up, at least try to knock out a couple of possible answers. Eliminate what you can and then guess at the remaining answer choices before moving on.

✓ Check Your Work

Since you will probably not know every term listed and the answer to every question, it is important that you get credit for the ones that you do know. Don't miss any questions through careless mistakes. If at all possible, try to take a second to look back over your answer selection and make sure you've selected the correct answer choice and haven't made a costly careless mistake (such as marking an answer choice that you didn't mean to mark). This quick double check should more than pay for itself in caught mistakes for the time it costs.

✓ PACE YOURSELF

It's easy to be overwhelmed when you're looking at a page full of questions; your mind is confused and full of random thoughts, and the clock is ticking down faster than you would like. Calm down and maintain the pace that you have set for yourself. Especially as you get down to the last few minutes of the test, don't let the small numbers on the clock make you panic. As long as you are on track by monitoring your pace, you are guaranteed to have time for each question.

✓ DON'T RUSH

It is very easy to make errors when you are in a hurry. Maintaining a fast pace in answering questions is pointless if it makes you miss questions that you would have gotten right otherwise. Test writers like to include distracting information and wrong answers that seem right. Taking a little extra time to avoid careless mistakes can make all the difference in your test score. Find a pace that allows you to be confident in the answers that you select.

✓ KEEP MOVING

Panicking will not help you pass the test, so do your best to stay calm and keep moving. Taking deep breaths and going through the answer elimination steps you practiced can help to break through a stress barrier and keep your pace.

Final Notes

The combination of a solid foundation of content knowledge and the confidence that comes from practicing your plan for applying that knowledge is the key to maximizing your performance on test day. As your foundation of content knowledge is built up and strengthened, you'll find that the strategies included in this chapter become more and more effective in helping you quickly sift through the distractions and traps of the test to isolate the correct answer.

Now that you're preparing to move forward into the test content chapters of this book, be sure to keep your goal in mind. As you read, think about how you will be able to apply this information on the test. If you've already seen sample questions for the test and you have an idea of the question format and style, try to come up with questions of your own that you can answer based on what you're reading. This will give you valuable practice applying your knowledge in the same ways you can expect to on test day.

Good luck and good studying!

Virtual Entry Assessment (VEA)

Overview

The Virtual Entry Assessment is self-administered and completed online as part of the application process to work for the United States Postal Service. Once you complete your job application, you will receive an email with a link to the required assessment; you will then have 72 hours (three days) from the time you receive the email to complete the assessment. The USPS recommends allowing 45 minutes with no distractions to complete all of the sections, although there is no time limit for any of the individual section. However, it may be to your benefit to complete each section as quickly as possible. If possible, take the assessment on a desktop or laptop computer rather than a tablet or mobile device to avoid technical complications; this may also be helpful as some of the text is rather small.

Applicants are ranked based on their scores, and only those at the top of the list will be offered a position. If you score below a 70%, you will be marked *Ineligible*, and you can retest again in 12 months. If you score above a 70% but want to retest to improve your score, you must wait 2 years before retaking the same test.

VEAs & Sections

In all, there are five sections, listed below, used in various combinations in the four Virtual Entry Assessments:

- **Work Scenarios** is a subjective assessment that contains situational judgment questions.
- **Tell Us Your Story** is a subjective assessment that contains a questionnaire that reviews your background and work experiences.
- **Describe Your Approach** is a subjective assessment similar to a personality test.
- **Error Checking** is an objective assessment that provides pairs of eight-digit numbers, which the test taker must decide are a match to each other or if the pairs contain an error.
- **Work Your Register** is an objective assessment that measures your ability to make change correctly and efficiently, using the fewest items of currency possible.

The four VEAs all contain the Work Scenarios, Tell Us Your Story, and Describe Your Approach sections. The assessments differ in the following ways:

- **VEA MC** or **Postal Exam 474** is for mail carrier candidates and includes no additional sections.
- **VEA MH** or **Postal Exam 475** is for mail handler candidates and also includes the Error Checking section.

- **VEA MP** or **Postal Exam 476** is for mail processor candidates and also includes the Error Checking section.
- **VEA CS** or **Postal Exam 477** is for customer service clerk candidates and also includes the Work Your Register section.

	Work Scenarios	Tell Us Your Story	Describe Your Approach	Error Checking	Work Your Register
VEA MC or Postal Exam 474	✓	✓	✓		
VEA MH or Postal Exam 475	✓	✓	✓	✓	
VEA MP or Postal Exam 476	✓	✓	✓	✓	
VEA CS or Postal Exam 477	✓	✓	✓		✓

Work Scenarios

Assessment	Number of Questions	Recommended Time to Complete Section
VEA MC or Postal Exam 474	8 questions	7 minutes
VEA MH or Postal Exam 475	9 questions	11 minutes
VEA MP or Postal Exam 476	9 questions	11 minutes
VEA CS or Postal Exam 477	10 questions	8 minutes

The Work Scenarios section appears in all four assessments of the postal exam series. There is not a stated time limit, but you are advised to complete this section as quickly as you can. As you are working, you may only go back one question, and once you answer a question, it will send you to the next, so you do not have unlimited navigation as you complete the section. Do not rush, and be deliberate with your selections. The types of questions for the 475 and 476 exams will vary based on the traits desirable for the associated positions.

Question Formatting

Work Scenarios is a situational judgment style assessment, and you will be given one- or two-sentence situations, such as those you might face on the job, and a selection of nuanced responses to each scenario. From the choices, you are to select how you are most and least likely to respond.

Note that these are not traditionally formatted multiple-choice questions; you will check one box in the *Most* column and one box in the *Least* column for the responses or actions you are most and least likely to take, respectively.

The example scenario will be described here.		
What you be most and least likely to do?		
Most	**←Pick one of each→**	**Least**
✓	Response 1	
	Response 2	
	Response 3	✓
	Response 4	

Many or all of the suggested responses given will be good choices. As you work through this section, you are to assess 1) what you personally would be most likely to do, and 2) the values, culture, and expectations of the USPS.

USPS Values

The entire application and assessment process for USPS positions emphasizes the importance of communication and teamwork. Regardless of which VEA you take, strong interpersonal skills are important, so be sure to emphasize how well you interact with others, even if you aren't applying for a customer service position.

The unofficial motto of the USPS is: "Neither snow nor rain nor heat nor gloom of night stays these couriers from the swift completion of their appointed rounds." Dedication, hard work, and going above and beyond the call of duty are all values important to the USPS. This applies in both teamwork and customer service; USPS employees are asked to actively search for ways to serve both customers and coworkers, and you should be willing to stop what you are working on and help a coworker or customer if asked.

Customer care is about more than just fixing a customer's problem; it also importantly involves making a customer feel that you care about their concerns and understand and empathize with their frustrations. Listening well and genuinely apologizing go a long way.

When considering situations and possible responses involving customers, take special note of a few things:

- Does the response address the customer's concern patiently or hastily?
- Can you go above and beyond for the customer within the bounds of your job description?
- How can you listen to the customer and make them feel heard as they tell you about their complaint?
- Can you help them solve their problem in a timely manner, especially if they are in a hurry?

In addition to customer care, the USPS also values efficiency and productivity. When considering possible responses to these theoretical work situations, keep this workplace value in mind. Wasted time and lost productivity should be avoided wherever possible.

EXAMPLES

The following examples represent the types and format of questions you will encounter on this section of the assessment. Paying careful attention to the values each response represents, select which response you are personally most and least likely to have. As this is a personality-style section, there are no right or wrong answers. However, some answers may better fit certain job descriptions. You should be familiar with the description of the job for which you are applying before you take the assessment.

It is very busy today, and you notice a few coworkers chatting in the corner instead of doing their work.		
What you be most and least likely to do?		
Most	**←Pick one of each→**	**Least**
	Keep your head down and keep working on your own tasks in order to meet your quota.	
	Tell your supervisor so that he can handle the situation.	
	Work harder to cover their productivity deficit.	
	Ask those coworkers to help out so that the workload is more manageable.	

Conflict such as this can be uncomfortable, but when working as part of a team, it can sometimes be necessary. Handling conflict and tension in a polite and gentle way directly with the offending party is a healthy way to address it. If that is unsuccessful, then address it with a supervisor.

You are in the middle of a project with a rapidly approaching deadline when a coworker asks for your help.		
What you be most and least likely to do?		
Most	**←Pick one of each→**	**Least**
	Drop what you are doing and help your coworker.	
	Politely ask the coworker to check if anyone else can help first.	
	Tell them you will help when you have completed your project.	
	Get to a good stopping point and jump in to help them.	

While the nuance of the response depends on you, a combination of both teamwork and mindfulness of productivity best reflects the values and culture of the USPS.

Tell Us Your Story

Assessment	Number of Questions	Recommended Time to Complete Section
VEA MC or Postal Exam 474	20 questions	2 minutes
VEA MH or Postal Exam 475	22 questions	3 minutes
VEA MP or Postal Exam 476	22 questions	3 minutes
VEA CS or Postal Exam 477	21 questions	2 minutes

Tell Us Your Story appears in all four assessments of the postal exam series. There is not a stated time limit, but you are advised to compete this section as quickly as you can. As you are working, you may only go back one question; once you answer a question, it will send you to the next, so you do not have unlimited navigation as you complete the section. Do not rush, and be deliberate with your selections. The types of questions for the 475 and 476 exams will vary based on the traits desirable for the associated positions.

These appear as traditional multiple-choice questions.

Work Experience Questions

The Tell Us Your Story section is described by USPS as examining your work experiences and background. Before you complete this section of the assessment, it would be helpful to thoroughly review the details of your resume and work history that you submitted on your job application. Many of the multiple-choice questions on this assessment will be based on information you submitted with your application and will be scored according to how truthful and accurate you are. For example, *In the last three years, how many of your jobs involved a productivity quota?* or *In the last three years, how many times did you resign voluntarily?*

These questions do have a right and wrong answer, and your answers must match the information you submitted. Before starting the assessment, review the dates and lengths of time you held each job; it may even be helpful to make a note of those timeframes. Consider which positions you left voluntarily and which you left involuntarily (were fired from).

If this will be your first job, that will be a provided answer choice on questions about your work history. The other answer choices will likely be number or time ranges: *0, 1–2, 3–4, 5 or more* or *0–6 months, 6 months–2 years, 2–4 years, 4–6 years, longer than 6 years.*

Professionalism Questions

Tell Us Your Story also includes more subjective questions about your interpersonal skills, professionalism, and attendance.

Unexcused or unannounced tardiness and absences have no place in a professional work environment, except in rare emergencies. Hopefully your work record reflects this and your listed references will agree, and questions about tardiness or absences should be answered accordingly. However, be honest: If you have a history of being late or not showing up for work and the people you listed as references know this, your answers on this section could be compared to the responses given by your references. Honesty and self-awareness matter.

While it may be tempting to answer many of these questions as if you were a perfect person, a better approach is to answer them with an honest assessment of your best self. As with other sections, it is important to remember that the USPS values teamwork, clear verbal communication, and strong interpersonal skills. Many of these types of questions will ask how your past coworkers and supervisors would rate those skills compared to others.

If asked about how well you follow an organization's policies and procedures, remember that the USPS values both. Also note the tone and extremity of how a question is worded; *What do you think about ____?* is a very different question than one that asks how many times you were formally disciplined for violating that same thing. For example, compare:

- How many times a year is it acceptable to be tardy?
- How many times have you been formally disciplined for being tardy?

There is a little room to give a less extreme, more nuanced answer (that accounts for the fact that no one is perfect) on a question worded like the first, with an answer such as, "It is okay if it happens very rarely." However, the question about being formally disciplined should be answered giving the fewest instances that are honestly possible. Having a history of violating company policy such that a formal reprimand is required is not something the USPS will look for in an employee.

Whether you are applying for a temporary position or a permanent position, if you are asked how long you intend to work for USPS, give an optimistically long time frame. Hiring and training employees is expensive, and indicating you are interested in sticking around shows that you are an ambitious, motivated, and committed candidate worth investing in. If you are applying for a permanent position, do not give an answer of less than 2 years.

Describe Your Approach

Assessment	Number of Questions	Recommended Time to Complete Section
VEA MC or Postal Exam 474	56 questions	6 minutes
VEA MH or Postal Exam 475	79 questions	8 minutes
VEA MP or Postal Exam 476	79 questions	8 minutes
VEA CS or Postal Exam 477	56 questions	6 minutes

The Describe Your Approach section appears in all four of the postal exam series. There is not a stated time limit, but you are advised to complete this section as quickly as you can. As you are working, you may only go back one question, and once you answer a question, it will send you to the next, so you do not have unlimited navigation as you complete the section. Do not rush, and be deliberate with your selections. The types of questions for the 475 and 476 exams will vary based on the traits desirable for the associated positions.

Describe Your Approach is a subjective personality-style test, but that doesn't mean it can't be used to screen out candidates. The section introduction states that it is designed to get to know your work style and approach to work in general; the unwritten purpose, however, is to make sure your personality matches the position to which you have applied. While there are typically no wrong answers to individual questions, attempting to answer questions so that you appear to be a perfect person can cause the section to be flagged as dishonest or suspect. No one is perfect; answer the questions honestly as your best self.

Question Formatting

Each question will consist of two seemingly opposite descriptive statements and four answer choices. You are to select whether the top or bottom statement is most or somewhat like you. On the assessment, the white sections are each of the answer choices, and they refer to the statement above or below, as indicated by the corresponding arrows.

I consider myself to be an optimist.
↑ Most like me
↑ Somewhat like me
↓ Somewhat like me
↓ Most like me
I consider myself to be a realist.

Read the Job Description

Each question supposes that there is a trade-off in a person between the traits described in the two statements, which may or may not be true. In this example, it is desirable in the workplace to both honor deadlines and work with excellence, but some jobs may require more of one trait than another. Be sure to read the job description of the position for which you applied before completing this section, as it may give you an indication of which of your traits and strengths to emphasize more.

I prefer to complete projects on time.
↑ Most like me
↑ Somewhat like me
↓ Somewhat like me
↓ Most like me
I prefer to complete projects to the best of my ability.

Other important things to note in the job description:

- Does the job involve a lot of routine or will it require adapting to new things frequently?
- Does the job include quotas and deadlines or more customer care and interpersonal interaction?

USPS Values

The entire application and assessment process for USPS positions emphasizes the importance of communication and teamwork. Regardless of which VEA you take, strong interpersonal skills are important, so be sure to emphasize how well you interact with others, even if you aren't applying for a customer service position.

The unofficial motto of the USPS is: "Neither snow nor rain nor heat nor gloom of night stays these couriers from the swift completion of their appointed rounds." Dedication, hard work, and going above and beyond the call of duty are all values important to the USPS.

Be Consistent

As you are completing the Describe Your Approach section, you will notice the repetition of wording and themes in the questions. Keeping the job description in mind, be sure to answer as consistently as possible. Consider yourself an optimist? Stick with that answer every time the statements ask about it. Think that success is about hard work and not luck? Do you think it is more important to try your best or to reach your goals? Be consistent as you answer questions with various ways of wording those choices.

Note Strong Wording

Pay attention to strong wording. No one is perfect, so carefully consider selecting the *Most like me* option when generalizations such as *never* (or *always*) are used. In the example, even though the top statement uses the word *sometimes*, *rude* is a strong, negative word, and although everyone has bad days, being rude to others is never a good thing. The use of strong, negative words (such as *frustrated* or *angry*) should be a clue that the assessment views a statement as a negative trait.

I can sometimes respond rudely to others.
↑ Most like me
↑ Somewhat like me
↓ Somewhat like me
↓ Most like me
I am never rude to others.

Avoid Extremes

Selecting *Most like me* should be done rarely. The two statements given will not usually have a clearly good or bad answer, so it is safest to stick with *Somewhat like me* most of the time, and only use *Most like me* when you are absolutely sure that the trait described is best for the position, aligns with USPS values, and describes you well.

Examples

I work best in an organized environment.
↑ Most like me
↑ Somewhat like me
↓ Somewhat like me
↓ Most like me
I work best in a fast-paced environment.

When both statements seem positive after reading them closely, or both options seem to apply to the USPS work environment, it may be best to select a *Somewhat like me* answer rather than a *Most like me* answer. For example, the USPS is both fast-paced and organized, so indicating that you strongly prefer one to the other probably won't help your score.

I prefer to work independently.
↑ Most like me
↑ Somewhat like me
↓ Somewhat like me
↓ Most like me
I work well when monitored by a supervisor.

Knowing which of the *Somewhat like me* answers is best will depend on the description of the job for which you are applying; in a mail processing facility, your position may involve more supervision by your boss; on a mail route, it may involve less. For most positions, you should avoid the *Most like me* answers when the statements assess supervision versus independence in your work preferences. To be successful on questions like this, it is important to know the description of the job for which you are applying.

Check for Errors

Assessment	Number of Questions	Recommended Time to Complete Section
VEA MC or Postal Exam 474	Not in this assessment	Not in this assessment
VEA MH or Postal Exam 475	3 tasks (12 number sets)	2 minutes
VEA MP or Postal Exam 476	3 tasks (12 number sets)	2 minutes
VEA CS or Postal Exam 477	Not in this assessment	Not in this assessment

In the Check for Errors section of the 475 and 476 Assessments, you will be given pairs of eight-digit numbers to compare, and you must determine if they are a **match** (the two eight-digit numbers are exactly the same) or if they contain an **error** (the two eight-digit numbers are not exactly the same).

Question Formatting

These are not traditional multiple choice-style questions. The number pairs will appear in a table; for each location in a table, you will be comparing the Original ID to the Computer ID and checking a box to indicate whether the number pair contains a Match or an Error.

In this example, the first number pair is labelled *Location A*: 84263579 is the Original ID and 84263679 is the Computer ID. The sixth digits (a 5 and a 6) do not match, so you should indicate the error by checking the *Error* column for the *Location A* row.

	Original ID	Computer ID	Match?	Error?
Location A	84263579	84263679		
Location B	24753680	24753680		
Location C	01593576	01593876		
Location D	96325874	96326874		

Examples

It may be helpful to visually isolate one number pair at a time so that you don't accidentally consider visually similar digits or identical digits from the wrong set when you are working quickly. Also be careful of various digits that appear similar to each other. For example, 3s and 8s may look similar, and if a zero appears with a slash through it (Ø), be careful not to confuse it with an 8.

Examining the eight-digit numbers in smaller pieces—two, three, or four digits at a time—may also be helpful when checking for errors. For example, 35487315 can be broken up as 35-48-73-15, 354-873-15, or 3548-7315, depending on your preference. It may be best to start by comparing digits two at a time and slowly working towards larger digit sets as you get more comfortable with this type of question and the size, font, and spacing of the numbers being used in the question.

Example 1: For each location below, select Match or Error based on the location information.

	Original ID	Computer ID	Match?	Error?
Location A	84263579	84263679		
Location B	24753680	24753680		
Location C	01593576	01593876		
Location D	96325874	96326874		

Example 2: For each location below, select Match or Error based on the location information.

	Original ID	Computer ID	Match?	Error?
Location A	88896354	88696354		
Location B	88975869	88897569		
Location C	88885348	88885348		
Location D	88957483	88957483		

Example 3: For each location below, select Match or Error based on the location information.

	Original ID	Computer ID	Match?	Error?
Location A	98563210	98563210		
Location B	96325874	96235874		
Location C	98645225	96845225		
Location D	96784550	96784550		

Example 1: Answers

	Original ID	Computer ID	Match?	Error?
Location A	84263579	84263679		✓
Location B	24753680	24753680	✓	
Location C	01593576	01593876		✓
Location D	96325874	96326874		✓

Example 2: Answers

	Original ID	Computer ID	Match?	Error?
Location A	88896354	88696354		✓
Location B	88975869	88897569		✓
Location C	88885348	88885348	✓	
Location D	88957483	88957483	✓	

Example 3: Answers

	Original ID	Computer ID	Match?	Error?
Location A	98563210	98563210	✓	
Location B	96325874	96235874		✓
Location C	98645225	96845225		✓
Location D	96784550	96784550	✓	

Work Your Register

Assessment	Number of Questions	Recommended Time to Complete Section
VEA MC or Postal Exam 474	Not in this assessment	Not in this assessment
VEA MH or Postal Exam 475	Not in this assessment	Not in this assessment
VEA MP or Postal Exam 476	Not in this assessment	Not in this assessment
VEA CS or Postal Exam 477	3 questions	2 minutes

The Work Your Register section only appears on the Virtual Entry Assessment CS 477, also known as the Customer Service VEA Exam. There are only three questions, and there is no section time limit, although the time frame of 2 minutes is recommended. It may be beneficial to work as quickly as you can while still being accurate. You are allowed to use a calculator if you would like.

Given a graphical representation of a cash drawer, you will be asked to determine the most efficient way to make exact change using the fewest items of currency (bills and coins) possible. Always start with the largest denomination available (usually 20-dollar bills), and work your way through the currency to pennies to ensure you are using the fewest number of bills and coins.

You will not be asked to calculate the change owed, but you will be given information you don't need: the amount paid and the amount the customer owes. However, the change due to the customer will also be given, and your only task is to calculate the most efficient way to make that change. Just be sure you read carefully so that you know which given dollar amount you are making change for.

Making Change Efficiently

You should first be comfortable making change efficiently. For example, if you owe a customer $24.63 in change, first determine how many $20s you will need, then $10s, then $5s, then $1s, then quarters, dimes, nickels, and finally pennies.

- $20s: 1
- $10s: 0
- $5s: 0
- $1s: 4
- Quarters ($0.25): 2
- Dimes ($0.10): 1
- Nickels ($0.05): 0
- Pennies ($0.01): 3

Check your answer by adding up the amounts:

$$(1 \times \$20) + (4 \times \$1) + (2 \times \$0.25) + (1 \times \$0.10) + (3 \times \$0.01) = \$24.63$$

Example: A customer rings up for $36.74 and pays with 2 twenty-dollar bills, so you owe them $3.26. If you make change with the fewest items of currency possible, how many five-dollar bills will you give them?

- $20s: 0
- $10s: 0
- $5s: 0
- $1s: 3
- Quarters ($0.25): 1
- Dimes ($0.10): 0
- Nickels ($0.05): 0
- Pennies ($0.01): 1

Because you only owe the customer $3.26 in change, you will not need any five-dollar bills. Check your answer by adding up the amounts:

$$(3 \times \$1) + (1 \times \$0.25) + (1 \times \$0.01) = \$3.26$$

Example: You owe a customer $10.95 in change after they paid you with a twenty-dollar bill. If you make change with the fewest items of currency possible, how many dimes will you give them?

- $20s: 0
- $10s: 1
- $5s: 0
- $1s: 0
- Quarters ($0.25): 3
- Dimes ($0.10): 2
- Nickels ($0.05): 0
- Pennies ($0.01): 0

You will give the customer two dimes. Check your answer by adding up the amounts:

$$(1 \times \$10) + (3 \times \$0.25) + (2 \times \$0.10) = \$10.95$$

Question Formatting

One of the challenges of this assessment section is getting comfortable with the question formatting. Rather than a traditional multiple-choice question, you will be given a graphical representation of a cash drawer which you will use to submit your answer.

Example: Make change for the following transaction using the fewest bills and coins.

Transaction Total: $24.67 Amount Paid: $30.00 Change Due: $5.33			
0	0	0	0
$20	$10	$5	$1
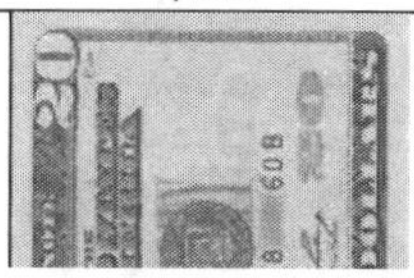		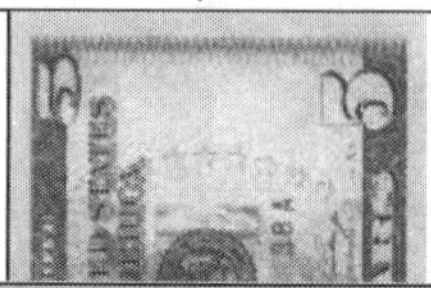	
0	0	0	0
$0.25	$0.10	$0.05	$0.01

Each bolded cell with a 0 in it is the field where you will submit your answer; below that is the type of currency for that field; below that is a picture of the top of the bill or the coin for that item of currency.

Rather than using your keyboard, when you click on the bolded cell with the 0, the digits 0–9 will appear, and you will select the appropriate response:

0	1	2	3	4
5	6	7	8	9

The completed example above will look like this:

Transaction Total: $24.67 Amount Paid: $30.00 Change Due: $5.33			
0	0	1	0
$20	$10	$5	$1
1	0	1	3
$0.25	$0.10	$0.05	$0.01

Ignoring the transaction total and amount paid, the number of each item of currency needed to make the $5.33 change due is:

- $20s: 0
- $10s: 0
- $5s: 1
- $1s: 0
- Quarters ($0.25): 1
- Dimes ($0.10): 0
- Nickels ($0.05): 1
- Pennies ($0.01): 3

Postal Exam Practice Test

Work Scenarios

Assessment	Number of Questions	Recommended Time to Complete Section
VEA MC or Postal Exam 474	8 questions	7 minutes
VEA MH or Postal Exam 475	9 questions	11 minutes
VEA MP or Postal Exam 476	9 questions	11 minutes
VEA CS or Postal Exam 477	10 questions	8 minutes

Depending on the VEA you take, the Work Scenarios section will have 8, 9, or 10 questions to be completed as quickly as you can. The situations will be tailored to the position you are applying for, but they will all have a similar theme and format.

1. Using the given scenario, select how you are most and least likely to respond.

A customer approaches your register and says that the item she needs appears to be out of stock and they need it urgently.		
What you be most and least likely to do?		
Most	**←Pick one of each→**	**Least**
	Apologize that it is out of stock and suggest she check the USPS website or another store in town.	
	Inquire what the customer needs the product for and suggest a suitable substitute that is in stock.	
	Give her the locations and addresses of other nearby USPS stores that show the item in stock.	
	Check the restock date and politely let the customer know when it will be back in stock.	

2. Using the given scenario, select how you are most and least likely to respond.

You are about to take a break when you notice another team seems to have work piled up.		
What you be most and least likely to do?		
Most	**←Pick one of each→**	**Least**
	Take your break and check on them when you come back and assist if you can.	
	Let your supervisor know about the delay and ask if you can help. Take your break a little later than planned.	
	Inform the supervisor of the other team about the delay.	
	Verbally encourage the other team as you go take your break; you know how hard it can be to catch up.	

3. Using the given scenario, select how you are most and least likely to respond.

You are in the middle of an important task due at the end of the day when a team member asks you for help with something they are working on.		
What you be most and least likely to do?		
Most	**←Pick one of each→**	**Least**
	Get to a stopping point and help them with what they need.	
	Ask them to check with others for assistance, and you will help if they can't find anyone else.	
	Drop what you are working on and help them so that they don't lose productivity.	
	Let them know you are working on something urgent, and you'll help them when you are finished.	

4. Using the given scenario, select how you are most and least likely to respond.

A machine on your line has gone down, and the technician will be there in 1–2 hours.		
What you be most and least likely to do?		
Most	**←Pick one of each→**	**Least**
	Take your lunch break now and hope that the technician has arrived when you get back.	
	Divide your work among a few other lines and join one of them to prevent a backlog while you wait.	
	Leave a message with your supervisor and wait to take action until you hear from her.	
	Tidy up your work area while you wait for the technician; take your lunch break when they arrive.	

5. Using the given scenario, select how you are most and least likely to respond.

A customer on your delivery route makes a complaint about the person who took your place while you were out of town last week.		
What you be most and least likely to do?		
Most	**←Pick one of each→**	**Least**
	Listen to them attentively and apologize on behalf of your team.	
	Give them your supervisor's number if they would like to make a formal complaint.	
	Apologize and ask if there is anything you can do to make it right.	
	Let your coworker and supervisor know about the complaint after listening attentively.	

6. Using the given scenario, select how you are most and least likely to respond.

You are delivering mail along your route when a customer asks you about a missing package.		
What you be most and least likely to do?		
Most	**←Pick one of each→**	**Least**
	Give them the website where they can report the missing package.	
	Explain the recent delays in the area and ask them to wait a few days because it may show up. Follow up with them in a few days.	
	Get information from them on when they expected it and if they have a tracking number, then show them how to report the missing package, if necessary.	
	Call the processing center for them to see if they have it there.	

7. Using the given scenario, select how you are most and least likely to respond.

The customer at your register asks a question for which you do not have an answer, but the line behind her is very long.		
What you be most and least likely to do?		
Most	**←Pick one of each→**	**Least**
	Look up or call to find the answer before moving on to the next customer.	
	Get her name and number and let her know you will contact her with the answer as soon as you get a chance.	
	Apologize that you don't have an answer and point her to the FAQ page of the website.	
	Ask her if she would like to wait for your supervisor to return to the counter so he can answer her question.	

8. Using the given scenario, select how you are most and least likely to respond.

A coworker you don't get along well with has started appearing frustrated and being consistently late to work.		
What you be most and least likely to do?		
Most	**←Pick one of each→**	**Least**
	Work harder to make up for their lost productivity.	
	Gently approach them to ask if everything is okay and see if you can help.	
	Quietly let your supervisor know that you are concerned that something may be going on in their personal life.	
	Politely mind your own business so that you don't offend them.	

9. Using the given scenario, select how you are most and least likely to respond.

You were recently assigned to work towards a quota with a less-than-motivated teammate.		
What you be most and least likely to do?		
Most	**←Pick one of each→**	**Least**
	Accept it and work as hard as you can to uphold your "half" of the quota.	
	Work hard to make up for any productivity deficits your partner may have.	
	Try to connect with and encourage your teammate, filling in the productivity gaps where necessary.	
	Discuss your concerns with your supervisor and ask to switch partners or be assigned to your own quota.	

10. Using the given scenario, select how you are most and least likely to respond.

It is an especially busy day, and you notice a coworker repeatedly on his phone during the shift.		
What you be most and least likely to do?		
Most	**←Pick one of each→**	**Least**
	Stay focused and keep working on your own tasks. It's always best to mind your own business.	
	Quietly let your supervisor know so that she can handle the situation.	
	Work harder to cover their productivity deficit. Maybe he has a lot going on at home right now.	
	Politely ask the coworker to help out so that the workload is more manageable.	

Tell Us Your Story

As this section of the VEAs contains questions created based on what you submitted in your application, the best way for you to practice and prepare for Tell Us Your Story is to review your work experience exactly as you submitted it on your application.

Describe Your Approach

1. Select which of the statements below is most or somewhat like you.

I am very self-motivated.
↑ Most like me
↑ Somewhat like me
↓ Somewhat like me
↓ Most like me
I work well as part of a team.

2. Select which of the statements below is most or somewhat like you.

Finishing a project on time is most important to me.
↑ Most like me
↑ Somewhat like me
↓ Somewhat like me
↓ Most like me
Finishing a project to the best of my ability is most important to me.

3. Select which of the statements below is most or somewhat like you.

I prefer a job with a variety of tasks.
↑ Most like me
↑ Somewhat like me
↓ Somewhat like me
↓ Most like me
I enjoy working based on routine.

4. Select which of the statements below is most or somewhat like you.

I have complete ownership of whether I fail or succeed.
↑ Most like me
↑ Somewhat like me
↓ Somewhat like me
↓ Most like me
Failure and success involve a little bit of luck.

5. Select which of the statements below is most or somewhat like you.

I am proud of my work ethic.
↑ Most like me
↑ Somewhat like me
↓ Somewhat like me
↓ Most like me
I am proud of my ability to relate to others.

6. Select which of the statements below is most or somewhat like you.

I am a great teammate.
↑ Most like me
↑ Somewhat like me
↓ Somewhat like me
↓ Most like me
I am a confident leader.

7. Select which of the statements below is most or somewhat like you.

At work, I enjoy completing assigned tasks.
↑ Most like me
↑ Somewhat like me
↓ Somewhat like me
↓ Most like me
At work, I enjoy solving new problems.

8. Select which of the statements below is most or somewhat like you.

I can sometimes be impatient.
↑ Most like me
↑ Somewhat like me
↓ Somewhat like me
↓ Most like me
I can sometimes be lazy.

9. Select which of the statements below is most or somewhat like you.

I rely on my good judgment to make a tough decision in the workplace.
↑ Most like me
↑ Somewhat like me
↓ Somewhat like me
↓ Most like me
I rely on my company's policies and procedures to make a tough decision in the workplace.

10. Select which of the statements below is most or somewhat like you.

I value accuracy.
↑ Most like me
↑ Somewhat like me
↓ Somewhat like me
↓ Most like me
I value speed.

11. Select which of the statements below is most or somewhat like you.

I am really creative.
↑ Most like me
↑ Somewhat like me
↓ Somewhat like me
↓ Most like me
I am really hardworking.

12. Select which of the statements below is most or somewhat like you.

I make decisions quickly and confidently.
↑ Most like me
↑ Somewhat like me
↓ Somewhat like me
↓ Most like me
I make decisions slowly and thoughtfully.

13. Select which of the statements below is most or somewhat like you.

It is sometimes okay to hold a grudge.
↑ Most like me
↑ Somewhat like me
↓ Somewhat like me
↓ Most like me
It is sometimes okay to get revenge.

14. Select which of the statements below is most or somewhat like you.

I work well with supervision.
↑ Most like me
↑ Somewhat like me
↓ Somewhat like me
↓ Most like me
I work well independently.

15. Select which of the statements below is most or somewhat like you.

I am in control of my emotions.
↑ Most like me
↑ Somewhat like me
↓ Somewhat like me
↓ Most like me
I often make decisions based on my emotions.

16. Select which of the statements below is most or somewhat like you.

I love helping my teammates.
↑ Most like me
↑ Somewhat like me
↓ Somewhat like me
↓ Most like me
I love working alone.

17. Select which of the statements below is most or somewhat like you.

I am very friendly.
↑ Most like me
↑ Somewhat like me
↓ Somewhat like me
↓ Most like me
I am very responsible.

18. Select which of the statements below is most or somewhat like you.

I am very careful.
↑ Most like me
↑ Somewhat like me
↓ Somewhat like me
↓ Most like me
I am very confident.

19. Select which of the statements below is most or somewhat like you.

I am very detail-oriented.
↑ Most like me
↑ Somewhat like me
↓ Somewhat like me
↓ Most like me
I prefer to think about big picture ideas.

20. Select which of the statements below is most or somewhat like you.

I relate well to others.
↑ Most like me
↑ Somewhat like me
↓ Somewhat like me
↓ Most like me
I consider myself a strong leader.

Check for Errors

Practice Set 1: The Check for Errors section of VEA 475 and 476 consists of 12 number pairs organized into three questions or sets. While there is no time limit, it is recommended that you complete the next three questions in two minutes or less.

1. For each item below, select Match or Error based on the location information.

	Original ID	Computer ID	Match?	Error?
Location A	77888953	77889953		
Location B	86453132	86453132		
Location C	85431585	88531585		
Location D	98431565	98437565		

2. For each item below, select Match or Error based on the location information.

	Original ID	Computer ID	Match?	Error?
Location A	46876512	48876512		
Location B	89463215	89444215		
Location C	98746515	98746515		
Location D	11668453	11668453		

3. For each item below, select Match or Error based on the location information.

	Original ID	Computer ID	Match?	Error?
Location A	38764321	38764321		
Location B	98465891	98465881		
Location C	98764135	78764135		
Location D	15673548	15673548		

Practice Set 2: The Check for Errors section of VEA 475 and 476 consists of 12 number pairs organized into three questions or sets. While there is no time limit, it is recommended that you complete the next three questions in two minutes or less.

4. For each item below, select Match or Error based on the location information.

	Original ID	Computer ID	Match?	Error?
Location A	65489434	65489434		
Location B	63579875	63579875		
Location C	35486758	35486758		
Location D	84357210	84557210		

5. For each item below, select Match or Error based on the location information.

	Original ID	Computer ID	Match?	Error?
Location A	16579832	16570832		
Location B	16578936	16578946		
Location C	15687951	15687951		
Location D	17498785	17498795		

6. For each item below, select Match or Error based on the location information.

	Original ID	Computer ID	Match?	Error?
Location A	95162348	95162348		
Location B	48159260	48159260		
Location C	75389614	75386914		
Location D	14275886	14275386		

Practice Set 3: The Check for Errors section of VEA 475 and 476 consists of 12 number pairs organized into three questions or sets. While there is no time limit, it is recommended that you complete the next three questions in two minutes or less.

7. For each item below, select Match or Error based on the location information.

	Original ID	Computer ID	Match?	Error?
Location A	95162348	95163248		
Location B	86453132	86453132		
Location C	98746515	98746515		
Location D	86535487	86533487		

8. For each item below, select Match or Error based on the location information.

	Original ID	Computer ID	Match?	Error?
Location A	68786432	68786432		
Location B	65487516	65487516		
Location C	98732158	98782158		
Location D	65481315	65482315		

9. For each item below, select Match or Error based on the location information.

	Original ID	Computer ID	Match?	Error?
Location A	68745612	68745612		
Location B	98735128	98735128		
Location C	32579813	32579813		
Location D	86572354	86542354		

Practice Set 4: The Check for Errors section of VEA 475 and 476 consists of 12 number pairs organized into three questions or sets. While there is no time limit, it is recommended that you complete the next three questions in two minutes or less.

10. For each item below, select Match or Error based on the location information.

	Original ID	Computer ID	Match?	Error?
Location A	36925814	36925814		
Location B	74108523	74105823		
Location C	91370546	91370536		
Location D	82469510	82469510		

11. For each item below, select Match or Error based on the location information.

	Original ID	Computer ID	Match?	Error?
Location A	82095135	82059135		
Location B	15902675	15902675		
Location C	02583694	02588694		
Location D	98795102	98795102		

12. For each item below, select Match or Error based on the location information.

	Original ID	Computer ID	Match?	Error?
Location A	97643150	97643150		
Location B	04258931	04258931		
Location C	84269573	84269573		
Location D	71935820	71983520		

Practice Set 5: The Check for Errors section of VEA 475 and 476 consists of 12 number pairs organized into three questions or sets. While there is no time limit, it is recommended that you complete the next three questions in two minutes or less.

13. For each item below, select Match or Error based on the location information.

	Original ID	Computer ID	Match?	Error?
Location A	79426830	79429830		
Location B	46560348	46560348		
Location C	58372538	58372538		
Location D	26142805	26141805		

14. For each item below, select Match or Error based on the location information.

	Original ID	Computer ID	Match?	Error?
Location A	49439479	49437479		
Location B	11592838	11582838		
Location C	19176661	19177661		
Location D	15409077	15409077		

15. For each item below, select Match or Error based on the location information.

	Original ID	Computer ID	Match?	Error?
Location A	43456966	43456966		
Location B	46506376	46504376		
Location C	33268253	33268253		
Location D	64215069	64215169		

Practice Set 6: The Check for Errors section of VEA 475 and 476 consists of 12 number pairs organized into three questions or sets. While there is no time limit, it is recommended that you complete the next three questions in two minutes or less.

16. For each item below, select Match or Error based on the location information.

	Original ID	Computer ID	Match?	Error?
Location A	88652128	88653128		
Location B	56610418	56610418		
Location C	57870420	57870420		
Location D	69209826	69209826		

17. For each item below, select Match or Error based on the location information.

	Original ID	Computer ID	Match?	Error?
Location A	72444684	72444684		
Location B	95773686	95793686		
Location C	76378875	76368875		
Location D	72135969	72136969		

18. For each item below, select Match or Error based on the location information.

	Original ID	Computer ID	Match?	Error?
Location A	90900156	90900156		
Location B	68900552	68930552		
Location C	72094913	72094913		
Location D	51271014	51274014		

Practice Set 7: The Check for Errors section of VEA 475 and 476 consists of 12 number pairs organized into three questions or sets. While there is no time limit, it is recommended that you complete the next three questions in two minutes or less.

19. For each item below, select Match or Error based on the location information.

	Original ID	Computer ID	Match?	Error?
Location A	26982457	26982457		
Location B	94095062	94025062		
Location C	63272990	63272990		
Location D	44295107	44297107		

20. For each item below, select Match or Error based on the location information.

	Original ID	Computer ID	Match?	Error?
Location A	82128839	82129839		
Location B	68289006	68289006		
Location C	52907596	52907596		
Location D	28227723	28227723		

21. For each item below, select Match or Error based on the location information.

	Original ID	Computer ID	Match?	Error?
Location A	68567100	68566100		
Location B	73862981	73862781		
Location C	67846118	67846118		
Location D	16946105	16943105		

Practice Set 8: The Check for Errors section of VEA 475 and 476 consists of 12 number pairs organized into three questions or sets. While there is no time limit, it is recommended that you complete the next three questions in two minutes or less.

22. For each item below, select Match or Error based on the location information.

	Original ID	Computer ID	Match?	Error?
Location A	72498563	72498563		
Location B	39263392	39263392		
Location C	69523174	69523174		
Location D	99774702	99774602		

23. For each item below, select Match or Error based on the location information.

	Original ID	Computer ID	Match?	Error?
Location A	93923101	93923101		
Location B	40817887	40817887		
Location C	22224719	22224519		
Location D	76408391	76488391		

24. For each item below, select Match or Error based on the location information.

	Original ID	Computer ID	Match?	Error?
Location A	58931018	58931318		
Location B	21687895	21687895		
Location C	81617552	81607552		
Location D	72662730	72660730		

Practice Set 9: The Check for Errors section of VEA 475 and 476 consists of 12 number pairs organized into three questions or sets. While there is no time limit, it is recommended that you complete the next three questions in two minutes or less.

25. For each item below, select Match or Error based on the location information.

	Original ID	Computer ID	Match?	Error?
Location A	60817689	60817689		
Location B	74810718	74810718		
Location C	71289593	71289493		
Location D	19303877	19403877		

26. For each item below, select Match or Error based on the location information.

	Original ID	Computer ID	Match?	Error?
Location A	87291287	87291287		
Location B	88171963	88171963		
Location C	14336481	14336781		
Location D	33667181	33667381		

27. For each item below, select Match or Error based on the location information.

	Original ID	Computer ID	Match?	Error?
Location A	54740008	54740008		
Location B	20521722	20531722		
Location C	65652342	65632342		
Location D	85717802	85717802		

Practice Set 10: The Check for Errors section of VEA 475 and 476 consists of 12 number pairs organized into three questions or sets. While there is no time limit, it is recommended that you complete the next three questions in two minutes or less.

28. For each item below, select Match or Error based on the location information.

	Original ID	Computer ID	Match?	Error?
Location A	28632485	28632285		
Location B	19859026	19859026		
Location C	58403102	58401102		
Location D	39443515	39443715		

29. For each item below, select Match or Error based on the location information.

	Original ID	Computer ID	Match?	Error?
Location A	78238763	78238763		
Location B	91022709	91002709		
Location C	55733072	55723072		
Location D	57295524	57295524		

30. For each item below, select Match or Error based on the location information.

	Original ID	Computer ID	Match?	Error?
Location A	30549609	30559609		
Location B	34446110	34446110		
Location C	54662685	54665685		
Location D	47912729	47912729		

Practice Set 11: The Check for Errors section of VEA 475 and 476 consists of 12 number pairs organized into three questions or sets. While there is no time limit, it is recommended that you complete the next three questions in two minutes or less.

31. For each item below, select Match or Error based on the location information.

	Original ID	Computer ID	Match?	Error?
Location A	58331778	58321778		
Location B	55189381	55159381		
Location C	81644273	81634273		
Location D	75605336	75603336		

32. For each item below, select Match or Error based on the location information.

	Original ID	Computer ID	Match?	Error?
Location A	80408384	80408284		
Location B	61260887	61260787		
Location C	28797509	28799509		
Location D	51416300	51516300		

33. For each item below, select Match or Error based on the location information.

	Original ID	Computer ID	Match?	Error?
Location A	53109373	53109373		
Location B	32143083	32142083		
Location C	91223224	91223224		
Location D	14552776	14552776		

Practice Set 12: The Check for Errors section of VEA 475 and 476 consists of 12 number pairs organized into three questions or sets. While there is no time limit, it is recommended that you complete the next three questions in two minutes or less.

34. For each item below, select Match or Error based on the location information.

	Original ID	Computer ID	Match?	Error?
Location A	11809006	11829006		
Location B	15568587	15568587		
Location C	82160507	82160507		
Location D	53454595	53454595		

35. For each item below, select Match or Error based on the location information.

	Original ID	Computer ID	Match?	Error?
Location A	34467731	34497731		
Location B	11171247	11181247		
Location C	79770614	79790614		
Location D	20367640	20367640		

36. For each item below, select Match or Error based on the location information.

	Original ID	Computer ID	Match?	Error?
Location A	97562674	97562674		
Location B	32604914	32624914		
Location C	62193067	62193067		
Location D	99088502	99098502		

Practice Set 13: The Check for Errors section of VEA 475 and 476 consists of 12 number pairs organized into three questions or sets. While there is no time limit, it is recommended that you complete the next three questions in two minutes or less.

37. For each item below, select Match or Error based on the location information.

	Original ID	Computer ID	Match?	Error?
Location A	12311507	12311507		
Location B	36729898	36749898		
Location C	70719704	70729704		
Location D	13693222	13692222		

38. For each item below, select Match or Error based on the location information.

	Original ID	Computer ID	Match?	Error?
Location A	49022344	49022344		
Location B	80569455	80569455		
Location C	22832563	22832563		
Location D	32762781	32762681		

39. For each item below, select Match or Error based on the location information.

	Original ID	Computer ID	Match?	Error?
Location A	38196223	38196223		
Location B	17818696	17818796		
Location C	29683817	29683717		
Location D	93146096	93145096		

Practice Set 14: The Check for Errors section of VEA 475 and 476 consists of 12 number pairs organized into three questions or sets. While there is no time limit, it is recommended that you complete the next three questions in two minutes or less.

40. For each item below, select Match or Error based on the location information.

	Original ID	Computer ID	Match?	Error?
Location A	77239168	77229168		
Location B	42328437	42338437		
Location C	49125799	49125799		
Location D	53109485	53109485		

41. For each item below, select Match or Error based on the location information.

	Original ID	Computer ID	Match?	Error?
Location A	27753362	27783362		
Location B	59506846	59506846		
Location C	67398900	67388900		
Location D	29121080	29141080		

42. For each item below, select Match or Error based on the location information.

	Original ID	Computer ID	Match?	Error?
Location A	49033789	49035789		
Location B	46429221	46429421		
Location C	26877631	26879631		
Location D	28324624	28224624		

Practice Set 15: The Check for Errors section of VEA 475 and 476 consists of 12 number pairs organized into three questions or sets. While there is no time limit, it is recommended that you complete the next three questions in two minutes or less.

43. For each item below, select Match or Error based on the location information.

	Original ID	Computer ID	Match?	Error?
Location A	43015356	43015356		
Location B	85773680	85773680		
Location C	50993771	50993971		
Location D	45812892	45812892		

44. For each item below, select Match or Error based on the location information.

	Original ID	Computer ID	Match?	Error?
Location A	88073391	88072391		
Location B	83784310	83784310		
Location C	44343369	44343369		
Location D	21680327	21680227		

45. For each item below, select Match or Error based on the location information.

	Original ID	Computer ID	Match?	Error?
Location A	11684811	11686811		
Location B	96964470	96964170		
Location C	64054952	64053952		
Location D	48300787	48300787		

Practice Set 16: The Check for Errors section of VEA 475 and 476 consists of 12 number pairs organized into three questions or sets. While there is no time limit, it is recommended that you complete the next three questions in two minutes or less.

46. For each item below, select Match or Error based on the location information.

	Original ID	Computer ID	Match?	Error?
Location A	14392821	14392021		
Location B	78672967	78672967		
Location C	23157271	23158271		
Location D	67024446	67024446		

47. For each item below, select Match or Error based on the location information.

	Original ID	Computer ID	Match?	Error?
Location A	96981284	96981284		
Location B	70992418	70992418		
Location C	10638963	10628963		
Location D	19094600	19094600		

48. For each item below, select Match or Error based on the location information.

	Original ID	Computer ID	Match?	Error?
Location A	32136298	32166298		
Location B	45553898	45553898		
Location C	16633354	16633354		
Location D	15390014	15300014		

Work Your Register

The VEA will be completed on the computer. When practicing with a paper test, write your answer in the bolded cells next to the 0. This is where you will digitally submit your answers and allows for practicing how answers will be submitted on the computer assessment.

Practice Set 1: The Work Your Register section of VEA 477 consists of three questions. While there is no time limit, it is recommended that you complete the next three questions in two minutes or less.

1. Make change for the following transaction using the fewest bills and coins.

Transaction Total: $3.77 Amount Paid: $20.00 Change Due: $16.23			
0	0	0	0
$20	$10	$5	$1
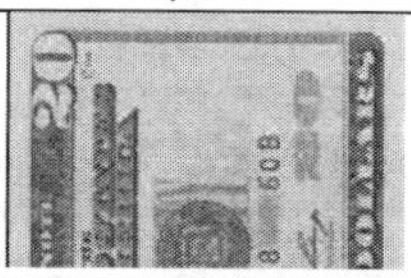			
0	0	0	0
$0.25	$0.10	$0.05	$0.01

2. Make change for the following transaction using the fewest bills and coins.

Transaction Total: $34.10 Amount Paid: $100.00 Change Due: $65.90			
0	0	0	0
$20	$10	$5	$1
0	0	0	0
$0.25	$0.10	$0.05	$0.01

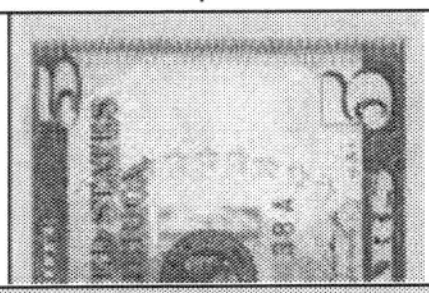

3. Make change for the following transaction using the fewest bills and coins.

Transaction Total: $6.80 Amount Paid: $10.00 Change Due: $3.20			
0	0	0	0
$20	$10	$5	$1
0	0	0	0
$0.25	$0.10	$0.05	$0.01

Practice Set 2: The Work Your Register section of VEA 477 consists of three questions. While there is no time limit, it is recommended that you complete the next three questions in two minutes or less.

4. Make change for the following transaction using the fewest bills and coins.

Transaction Total: $8.72 Amount Paid: $20.00 Change Due: $11.28			
0	0	0	0
$20	$10	$5	$1
0	0	0	0
$0.25	$0.10	$0.05	$0.01

5. Make change for the following transaction using the fewest bills and coins.

Transaction Total: $53.17 Amount Paid: $60.00 Change Due: $6.83			
0	0	0	0
$20	$10	$5	$1
0	0	0	0
$0.25	$0.10	$0.05	$0.01

6. Make change for the following transaction using the fewest bills and coins.

Transaction Total: $9.10 Amount Paid: $10.00 Change Due: $0.90			
0	0	0	0
$20	$10	$5	$1
0	0	0	0
$0.25	$0.10	$0.05	$0.01

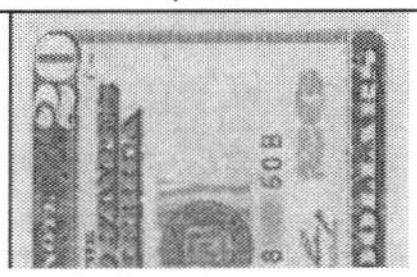

Practice Set 3: The Work Your Register section of VEA 477 consists of three questions. While there is no time limit, it is recommended that you complete the next three questions in two minutes or less.

7. Make change for the following transaction using the fewest bills and coins.

Transaction Total: $3.48
Amount Paid: $5.00
Change Due: $1.52

0	0	0	0
$20	$10	$5	$1
0	0	0	0
$0.25	$0.10	$0.05	$0.01

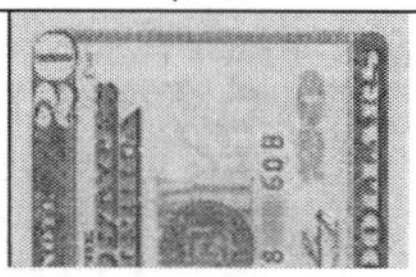

8. Make change for the following transaction using the fewest bills and coins.

Transaction Total: $9.23
Amount Paid: $10.00
Change Due: $0.77

0	0	0	0
$20	$10	$5	$1
0	0	0	0
$0.25	$0.10	$0.05	$0.01

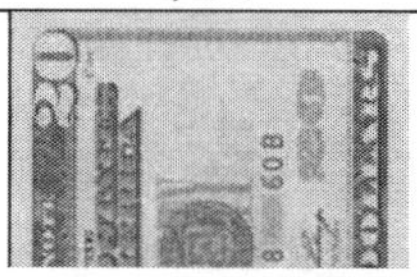

9. Make change for the following transaction using the fewest bills and coins.

Transaction Total: $70.13 Amount Paid: $100.00 Change Due: $29.87			
0	0	0	0
$20	$10	$5	$1
0	0	0	0
$0.25	$0.10	$0.05	$0.01

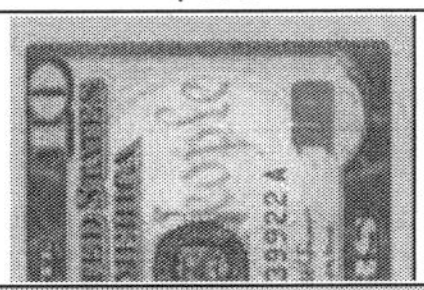

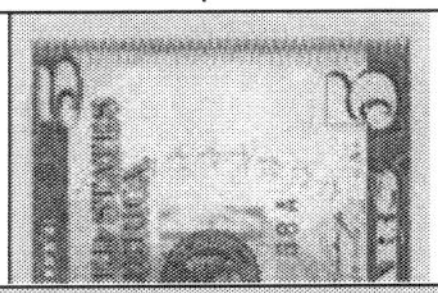

Practice Set 4: The Work Your Register section of VEA 477 consists of three questions. While there is no time limit, it is recommended that you complete the next three questions in two minutes or less.

10. Make change for the following transaction using the fewest bills and coins.

Transaction Total: $12.09 Amount Paid: $20.00 Change Due: $7.91			
0	0	0	0
$20	$10	$5	$1

0	0	0	0
$0.25	$0.10	$0.05	$0.01

11. Make change for the following transaction using the fewest bills and coins.

Transaction Total: $43.08 Amount Paid: $50.00 Change Due: $6.92			
0	0	0	0
$20	$10	$5	$1
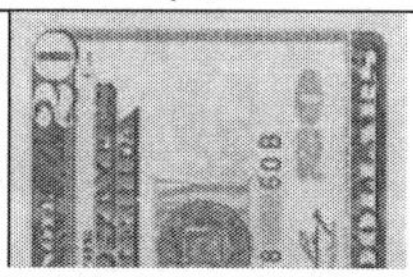		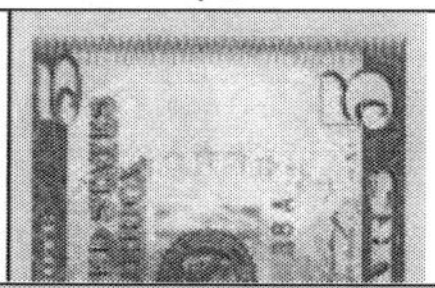	
0	0	0	0
$0.25	$0.10	$0.05	$0.01

12. Make change for the following transaction using the fewest bills and coins.

Transaction Total: $1.29 Amount Paid: $10.00 Change Due: $8.71			
0	0	0	0
$20	$10	$5	$1
0	0	0	0
$0.25	$0.10	$0.05	$0.01

Practice Set 5: The Work Your Register section of VEA 477 consists of three questions. While there is no time limit, it is recommended that you complete the next three questions in two minutes or less.

13. Make change for the following transaction using the fewest bills and coins.

Transaction Total: $20.67 Amount Paid: $30.00 Change Due: $9.33			
0	0	0	0
$20	$10	$5	$1
0	0	0	0
$0.25	$0.10	$0.05	$0.01

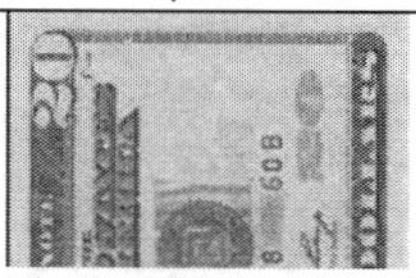

14. Make change for the following transaction using the fewest bills and coins.

Transaction Total: $47.72 Amount Paid: $60.00 Change Due: $12.28			
0	0	0	0
$20	$10	$5	$1
0	0	0	0
$0.25	$0.10	$0.05	$0.01

15. Make change for the following transaction using the fewest bills and coins.

Transaction Total: $25.48 Amount Paid: $26.00 Change Due: $0.52			
0	0	0	0
$20	$10	$5	$1
0	0	0	0
$0.25	$0.10	$0.05	$0.01

Practice Set 6: The Work Your Register section of VEA 477 consists of three questions. While there is no time limit, it is recommended that you complete the next three questions in two minutes or less.

16. Make change for the following transaction using the fewest bills and coins.

Transaction Total: $14.24
Amount Paid: $20.00
Change Due: $5.76

0	0	0	0
$20	$10	$5	$1
0	0	0	0
$0.25	$0.10	$0.05	$0.01

17. Make change for the following transaction using the fewest bills and coins.

Transaction Total: $52.46
Amount Paid: $70.00
Change Due: $17.54

0	0	0	0
$20	$10	$5	$1
0	0	0	0
$0.25	$0.10	$0.05	$0.01

18. Make change for the following transaction using the fewest bills and coins.

Transaction Total: $51.13 Amount Paid: $55.00 Change Due: $3.87			
0	0	0	0
$20	$10	$5	$1
0	0	0	0
$0.25	$0.10	$0.05	$0.01

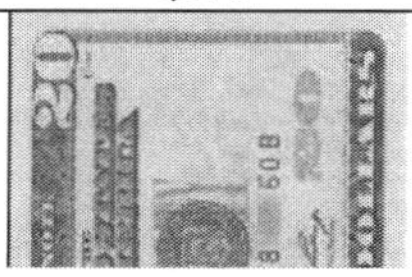

Practice Set 7: The Work Your Register section of VEA 477 consists of three questions. While there is no time limit, it is recommended that you complete the next three questions in two minutes or less.

19. Make change for the following transaction using the fewest bills and coins.

Transaction Total: $4.18 Amount Paid: $10.00 Change Due: $5.82			
0	0	0	0
$20	$10	$5	$1
		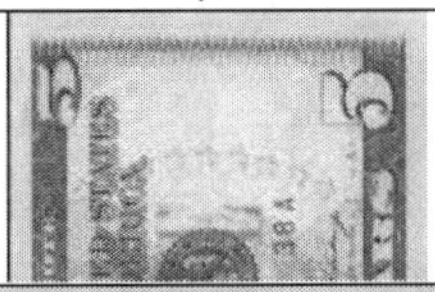	
0	0	0	0
$0.25	$0.10	$0.05	$0.01

20. Make change for the following transaction using the fewest bills and coins.

Transaction Total: $54.41 Amount Paid: $60.00 Change Due: $5.59			
0	0	0	0
$20	$10	$5	$1
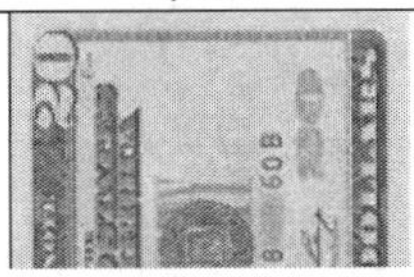			
0	0	0	0
$0.25	$0.10	$0.05	$0.01

21. Make change for the following transaction using the fewest bills and coins.

Transaction Total: $79.62 Amount Paid: $80.00 Change Due: $0.38			
0	0	0	0
$20	$10	$5	$1
0	0	0	0
$0.25	$0.10	$0.05	$0.01

Practice Set 8: The Work Your Register section of VEA 477 consists of three questions. While there is no time limit, it is recommended that you complete the next three questions in two minutes or less.

22. Make change for the following transaction using the fewest bills and coins.

Transaction Total: $86.86 Amount Paid: $100.00 Change Due: $13.14			
0	0	0	0
$20	$10	$5	$1
0	0	0	0
$0.25	$0.10	$0.05	$0.01

23. Make change for the following transaction using the fewest bills and coins.

Transaction Total: $70.94 Amount Paid: $80.00 Change Due: $9.06			
0	0	0	0
$20	$10	$5	$1
0	0	0	0
$0.25	$0.10	$0.05	$0.01

24. Make change for the following transaction using the fewest bills and coins.

Transaction Total: $21.60 Amount Paid: $50.00 Change Due: $28.40			
0	0	0	0
$20	$10	$5	$1
0	0	0	0
$0.25	$0.10	$0.05	$0.01

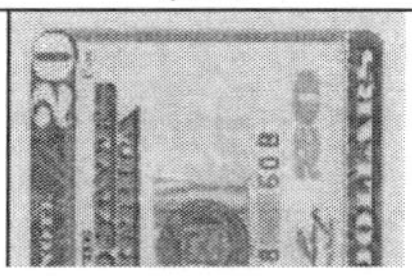

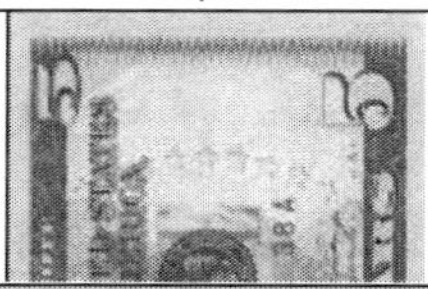

Practice Set 9: The Work Your Register section of VEA 477 consists of three questions. While there is no time limit, it is recommended that you complete the next three questions in two minutes or less.

25. Make change for the following transaction using the fewest bills and coins.

Transaction Total: $3.04
Amount Paid: $5.00
Change Due: $1.96

0	0	0	0
$20	$10	$5	$1
0	0	0	0
$0.25	$0.10	$0.05	$0.01

26. Make change for the following transaction using the fewest bills and coins.

Transaction Total: $76.98
Amount Paid: $100.00
Change Due: $23.02

0	0	0	0
$20	$10	$5	$1
0	0	0	0
$0.25	$0.10	$0.05	$0.01

27. Make change for the following transaction using the fewest bills and coins.

Transaction Total: $51.78 Amount Paid: $52.00 Change Due: $0.22			
0	0	0	0
$20	$10	$5	$1
0	0	0	0
$0.25	$0.10	$0.05	$0.01

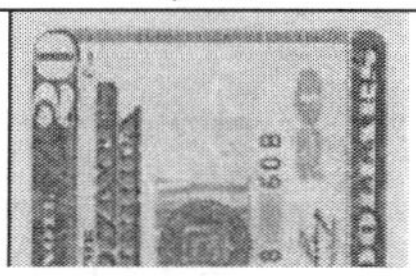

Practice Set 10: The Work Your Register section of VEA 477 consists of three questions. While there is no time limit, it is recommended that you complete the next three questions in two minutes or less.

28. Make change for the following transaction using the fewest bills and coins.

Transaction Total: $45.13
Amount Paid: $60.00
Change Due: $14.87

0	0	0	0
$20	$10	$5	$1
0	0	0	0
$0.25	$0.10	$0.05	$0.01

29. Make change for the following transaction using the fewest bills and coins.

Transaction Total: $30.32
Amount Paid: $40.00
Change Due: $9.68

0	0	0	0
$20	$10	$5	$1
0	0	0	0
$0.25	$0.10	$0.05	$0.01

30. Make change for the following transaction using the fewest bills and coins.

Transaction Total: $44.04
Amount Paid: $100.00
Change Due: $55.96

0	0	0	0
$20	$10	$5	$1
0	0	0	0
$0.25	$0.10	$0.05	$0.01

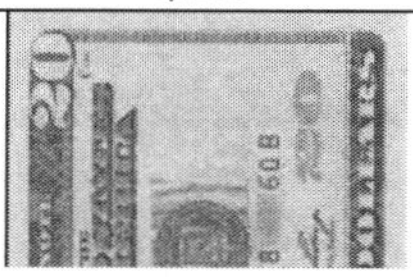

Practice Set 11: The Work Your Register section of VEA 477 consists of three questions. While there is no time limit, it is recommended that you complete the next three questions in two minutes or less.

31. Make change for the following transaction using the fewest bills and coins.

Transaction Total: $68.77 Amount Paid: $80.00 Change Due: $11.23			
0	0	0	0
$20	$10	$5	$1
0	0	0	0
$0.25	$0.10	$0.05	$0.01

32. Make change for the following transaction using the fewest bills and coins.

Transaction Total: $33.02 Amount Paid: $50.00 Change Due: $16.98			
0	0	0	0
$20	$10	$5	$1
0	0	0	0
$0.25	$0.10	$0.05	$0.01

33. Make change for the following transaction using the fewest bills and coins.

Transaction Total: $26.56 Amount Paid: $30.00 Change Due: $3.44			
0	0	0	0
$20	$10	$5	$1
0	0	0	0
$0.25	$0.10	$0.05	$0.01

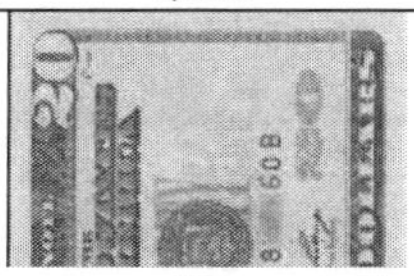

Practice Set 12: The Work Your Register section of VEA 477 consists of three questions. While there is no time limit, it is recommended that you complete the next three questions in two minutes or less.

34. Make change for the following transaction using the fewest bills and coins.

Transaction Total: $76.72
Amount Paid: $100.00
Change Due: $23.28

0	0	0	0
$20	$10	$5	$1
0	0	0	0
$0.25	$0.10	$0.05	$0.01

35. Make change for the following transaction using the fewest bills and coins.

Transaction Total: $2.83
Amount Paid: $5.00
Change Due: $2.17

0	0	0	0
$20	$10	$5	$1
0	0	0	0
$0.25	$0.10	$0.05	$0.01

36. Make change for the following transaction using the fewest bills and coins.

Transaction Total: $77.83 Amount Paid: $90.00 Change Due: $12.17			
0	0	0	0
$20	$10	$5	$1
0	0	0	0
$0.25	$0.10	$0.05	$0.01

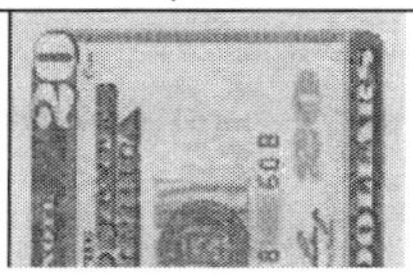

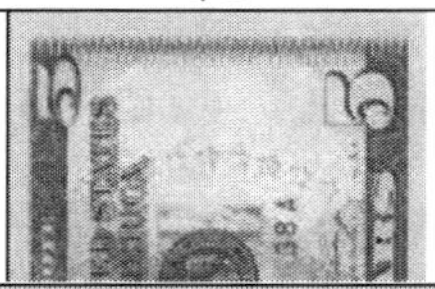

Practice Set 13: The Work Your Register section of VEA 477 consists of three questions. While there is no time limit, it is recommended that you complete the next three questions in two minutes or less.

37. Make change for the following transaction using the fewest bills and coins.

Transaction Total: $25.61
Amount Paid: $40.00
Change Due: $14.39

0	0	0	0
$20	$10	$5	$1
0	0	0	0
$0.25	$0.10	$0.05	$0.01

38. Make change for the following transaction using the fewest bills and coins.

Transaction Total: $17.42
Amount Paid: $20.00
Change Due: $2.58

0	0	0	0
$20	$10	$5	$1
0	0	0	0
$0.25	$0.10	$0.05	$0.01

39. Make change for the following transaction using the fewest bills and coins.

Transaction Total: $47.58 Amount Paid: $50.00 Change Due: $2.42			
0	0	0	0
$20	$10	$5	$1
0	0	0	0
$0.25	$0.10	$0.05	$0.01

Practice Set 14: The Work Your Register section of VEA 477 consists of three questions. While there is no time limit, it is recommended that you complete the next three questions in two minutes or less.

40. Make change for the following transaction using the fewest bills and coins.

Transaction Total: $61.88
Amount Paid: $80.00
Change Due: $18.12

0	0	0	0
$20	$10	$5	$1
0	0	0	0
$0.25	$0.10	$0.05	$0.01

41. Make change for the following transaction using the fewest bills and coins.

Transaction Total: $5.95
Amount Paid: $20.00
Change Due: $14.05

0	0	0	0
$20	$10	$5	$1
0	0	0	0
$0.25	$0.10	$0.05	$0.01

42. Make change for the following transaction using the fewest bills and coins.

Transaction Total: $49.92
Amount Paid: $50.00
Change Due: $0.08

0	0	0	0
$20	$10	$5	$1
0	0	0	0
$0.25	$0.10	$0.05	$0.01

Practice Set 15: The Work Your Register section of VEA 477 consists of three questions. While there is no time limit, it is recommended that you complete the next three questions in two minutes or less.

43. Make change for the following transaction using the fewest bills and coins.

Transaction Total: $25.76
Amount Paid: $30.00
Change Due: $4.24

0	0	0	0
$20	$10	$5	$1
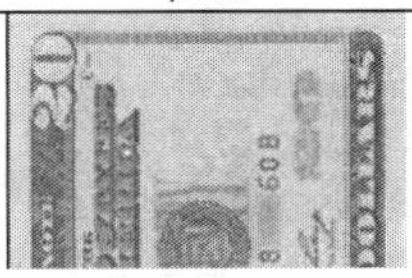			
0	0	0	0
$0.25	$0.10	$0.05	$0.01

44. Make change for the following transaction using the fewest bills and coins.

Transaction Total: $7.94
Amount Paid: $50.00
Change Due: $42.06

0	0	0	0
$20	$10	$5	$1
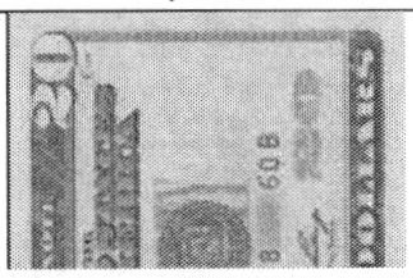			
0	0	0	0
$0.25	$0.10	$0.05	$0.01

45. Make change for the following transaction using the fewest bills and coins.

Transaction Total: $82.24 Amount Paid: $85.00 Change Due: $2.76			
0	0	0	0
$20	$10	$5	$1
0	0	0	0
$0.25	$0.10	$0.05	$0.01

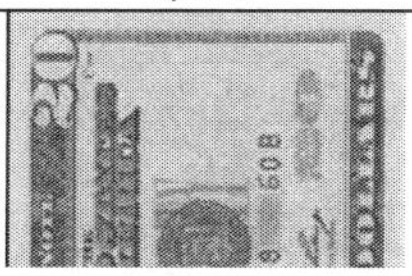

Practice Set 16: The Work Your Register section of VEA 477 consists of three questions. While there is no time limit, it is recommended that you complete the next three questions in two minutes or less.

46. Make change for the following transaction using the fewest bills and coins.

Transaction Total: $90.84 Amount Paid: $100.00 Change Due: $9.16			
0	0	0	0
$20	$10	$5	$1
0	0	0	0
$0.25	$0.10	$0.05	$0.01

47. Make change for the following transaction using the fewest bills and coins.

Transaction Total: $54.12 Amount Paid: $60.00 Change Due: $5.88			
0	0	0	0
$20	$10	$5	$1
0	0	0	0
$0.25	$0.10	$0.05	$0.01

48. Make change for the following transaction using the fewest bills and coins.

Transaction Total: $63.14 Amount Paid: $100.00 Change Due: $36.86			
0	0	0	0
$20	$10	$5	$1
0	0	0	0
$0.25	$0.10	$0.05	$0.01

Answer Key and Explanations

Work Scenarios

1. Best: Inquire what the customer needs the product for and suggest a suitable substitute that is in stock. This response demonstrated interest in the customer's needs and helps fix her problem as quickly as possible.

Worst: Check the restock date and politely let the customer know when it will be back in stock. This response makes no attempt to help the customer solve their problem in a timely manner.

2. Best: Let your supervisor know about the delay and ask if you can help. Take your break a little later than planned. This is the most helpful, productive, team-centered response.

Worst: Verbally encourage the other team as you go take your break; you know how hard it can be to catch up. While polite, this response does not demonstrate teamwork or contribute to the overall success of the facility.

3. Best: Ask them to check with others for assistance, and you will help if they can't find anyone else. This response best balances teamwork and the productivity of yourself and your teammate.

Worst: Let them know you are working on something urgent, and you'll help them when you are finished. This response does not demonstrate teamwork or contribute to the overall success of the facility.

4. Best: Divide your work among a few other lines and join one of them to prevent a backlog while you wait. This is the most team-oriented and productive response.

Worst: Take your lunch break now and hope that the technician has arrived when you get back. While there is only one good response on this list, taking your lunch break now and hoping the problem solves itself while you are gone is the least active, productive way to handle this scenario.

5. Best: Apologize and ask if there is anything you can do to make it right. This response contains the most customer-centric perspective of the responses.

Worst: Give them your supervisor's number if they would like to make a formal complaint. This is the most hands-off way to respond to the customer.

6. Best: Get information from them on when they expected it and if they have a tracking number, then show them how to report the missing package, if necessary. Taking an active role in helping to solve the customer's problem, if possible, is important. The customer will need to start the process themselves, but just giving them contact information to fix it themselves doesn't provide very much customer care.

Worst: Explain the recent delays in the area and ask them to wait a few days because it may show up. Follow up with them in a few days. This response makes no attempt to solve the customer's problem.

7. Best: Ask her if she would like to wait for your supervisor to return to the counter so he can answer her question. This response allows the customer's question to be answered as soon as possible while balancing the needs of the other customers who are waiting. If the customer turned down this option, following up with the offer to get her contact information and call her with an answer is a good alternative.

Worst: Apologize that you don't have an answer and point her to the FAQ page of the website. This is the least active way to help the customer with her question.

8. Best: Gently approach them to ask if everything is okay and see if you can help. While this may be the most uncomfortable response, it will let the teammate know that you care, even if you haven't gotten along in the past.

Worst: Politely mind your own business so that you don't offend them. This is the most passive response and the least helpful for the teammate and team dynamic.

9. Best: Try to connect with and encourage your teammate, filling in the productivity gaps where necessary. This is the most team-oriented response that balances productivity and a healthy team dynamic.

Worst: Accept it and work as hard as you can to uphold your "half" of the quota. This response does not involve working as a team at all.

10. Best: Politely ask the coworker to help out so that the workload is more manageable. Politely addressing the situation to prevent a slowdown is best, especially when a teammate appears to be violating company policy and doing personal things while on shift.

Worst: Stay focused and keep working on your own tasks. It's always best to mind your own business. Staying out of it without making up for the deficit neglects teamwork and productivity.

Describe Your Approach

1.

I am very self-motivated.	
↑ Most like me	
↑ Somewhat like me	
↓ Somewhat like me	✓
↓ Most like me	
I work well as part of a team.	

Both statements are positive, but since the USPS values teamwork, *I work well as part of a team/Somewhat like me* is the best answer.

2.

Finishing a project on time is most important to me.	
↑ Most like me	
↑ Somewhat like me	
↓ Somewhat like me	✓
↓ Most like me	
Finishing a project to the best of my ability is most important to me.	

Both statements are positive, but, for example, delivering a package to the wrong address will also make it late to the correct address, so *Finishing a project to the best of my ability is most important to me/ Somewhat like me* is the best answer.

3.

I prefer a job with a variety of tasks.	
↑ Most like me	
↑ Somewhat like me	✓
↓ Somewhat like me	✓
↓ Most like me	
I enjoy working based on routine.	

Depending on the job description, either *Somewhat like me* answer could be best.

4.

I have complete ownership of whether I fail or succeed.	
↑ Most like me	✓
↑ Somewhat like me	✓
↓ Somewhat like me	
↓ Most like me	
Failure and success involve a little bit of luck.	

In a work setting, taking ownership of your failures and successes is wise. Therefore, either option for *I have complete ownership of whether I fail or succeed* is good.

5.

I am proud of my work ethic.	
↑ Most like me	
↑ Somewhat like me	✓
↓ Somewhat like me	✓
↓ Most like me	
I am proud of my ability to relate to others.	

Depending on the job description, either *Somewhat like me* answer could be best. Teamwork and hard work are both important traits.

6.

I am a great teammate.	
↑ Most like me	
↑ Somewhat like me	✓
↓ Somewhat like me	
↓ Most like me	
I am a confident leader.	

Both statements are positive, but since the USPS values teamwork, *I am a great teammate/Somewhat like me* is the best answer.

7.

At work, I enjoy completing assigned tasks.	
↑ Most like me	
↑ Somewhat like me	✓
↓ Somewhat like me	
↓ Most like me	
At work, I enjoy solving new problems.	

Creative problem solving is an important skill, but most of the positions the Virtual Entry Assessments screen for involve completing assigned tasks; *At work, I enjoy completing assigned tasks/ Somewhat like me* is the best answer.

8.

I can sometimes be impatient.	
↑ Most like me	
↑ Somewhat like me	✓
↓ Somewhat like me	✓
↓ Most like me	
I can sometimes be lazy.	

Neither trait is very desirable, but nobody is perfect. Either *Somewhat like me* answer is good. Avoid the *Most like me* answers in questions like this.

9.

I rely on my good judgment to make a tough decision in the workplace.	
↑ Most like me	
↑ Somewhat like me	
↓ Somewhat like me	✓
↓ Most like me	
I rely on my company's policies and procedures to make a tough decision in the workplace.	

Good judgment is important, but so is following policy and procedure, especially in a large organization such as the USPS. *I rely on my company's policies and procedures to make a tough decision in the workplace/ Somewhat like me* is the best answer for a question like this.

10.

I value accuracy.	
↑ Most like me	
↑ Somewhat like me	✓
↓ Somewhat like me	
↓ Most like me	
I value speed.	

Both statements are positive, but, for example, delivering a package to the wrong address will also make it late to the correct address, so *I value accuracy/Somewhat like me* is the best answer.

11.

I am really creative.	
↑ Most like me	
↑ Somewhat like me	
↓ Somewhat like me	✓
↓ Most like me	✓
I am really hardworking.	

Creativity is not a bad thing, but as USPS positions require a good work ethic, *I am really creative/Most like me* is the worst answer, followed by *I am really creative/Somewhat like me*.

12.

I make decisions quickly and confidently.	
↑ Most like me	
↑ Somewhat like me	
↓ Somewhat like me	✓
↓ Most like me	
I make decisions slowly and thoughtfully.	

Confident, quick decision-making is a good skill, but thoughtful decision-making is more valuable. *I make decisions slowly and thoughtfully/Somewhat like me* is the best answer; the word *slowly* makes the *Most like me* option less desirable when applying for a position in a fast-paced work environment.

13.

It is sometimes okay to hold a grudge.	
↑ Most like me	
↑ Somewhat like me	✓
↓ Somewhat like me	
↓ Most like me	
It is sometimes okay to get revenge.	

Neither of these statements represent positive interpersonal skills, but getting revenge is more active and aggressive than holding a grudge, so *It is sometimes okay to hold a grudge/Somewhat like me* is the safest answer.

14.

I work well with supervision.	
↑ Most like me	
↑ Somewhat like me	✓
↓ Somewhat like me	✓
↓ Most like me	
I work well independently.	

Knowing which of the *Somewhat like me* answers is best will depend on the description of the job for which you are applying; in a mail processing facility, your position may involve more supervision by your boss; on a mail route, it may involve less. For most positions, you should avoid the *Most like me* answers when the statements assess supervision versus independence in your work preferences.

15.

I am in control of my emotions.	
↑ Most like me	✓
↑ Somewhat like me	✓
↓ Somewhat like me	
↓ Most like me	
I often make decisions based on my emotions.	

Being in control of your emotions is an important job skill, so either answer for *I am in control of my emotions* is preferable.

16.

I love helping my teammates.	
↑ Most like me	✓
↑ Somewhat like me	✓
↓ Somewhat like me	
↓ Most like me	
I love working alone.	

Teamwork is valued in USPS work culture, so either answer for *I love helping my teammates* is preferable.

17.

I am very friendly.	
↑ Most like me	
↑ Somewhat like me	✓
↓ Somewhat like me	✓
↓ Most like me	
I am very responsible.	

Both statements are positive, so either *Somewhat like me* answer is preferable to *Most like me.*

18.

I am very careful.	
↑ Most like me	✓
↑ Somewhat like me	✓
↓ Somewhat like me	
↓ Most like me	
I am very confident.	

Both statements are positive, but as USPS positions require attention to detail, either option for *I am very careful* is preferable.

19.

I am very detail-oriented.	
↑ Most like me	✓
↑ Somewhat like me	✓
↓ Somewhat like me	
↓ Most like me	
I prefer to think about big picture ideas.	

Both statements are positive, but as USPS positions require attention to detail, either option for *I am very careful* is preferable.

20.

I relate well to others.	
↑ Most like me	✓
↑ Somewhat like me	✓
↓ Somewhat like me	
↓ Most like me	
I consider myself a strong leader.	

Both statements are positive, but as USPS values teamwork, either option for *I relate well to others* is acceptable.

Check for Errors

1. For each item below, select Match or Error based on the location information.

	Original ID	Computer ID	Match?	Error?
Location A	77888953	77889953		✓
Location B	86453132	86453132	✓	
Location C	85431585	88531585		✓
Location D	98431565	98437565		✓

2. For each item below, select Match or Error based on the location information.

	Original ID	Computer ID	Match?	Error?
Location A	46876512	48876512		✓
Location B	89463215	89444215		✓
Location C	98746515	98746515	✓	
Location D	11668453	11668453	✓	

3. For each item below, select Match or Error based on the location information.

	Original ID	Computer ID	Match?	Error?
Location A	38764321	38764321	✓	
Location B	98465891	98465881		✓
Location C	98764135	78764135		✓
Location D	15673548	15673548	✓	

4. For each item below, select Match or Error based on the location information.

	Original ID	Computer ID	Match?	Error?
Location A	65489434	65489434	✓	
Location B	63579875	63579875	✓	
Location C	35486758	35486758	✓	
Location D	84357210	84557210		✓

5. For each item below, select Match or Error based on the location information.

	Original ID	Computer ID	Match?	Error?
Location A	16579832	16570832		✓
Location B	16578936	16578946		✓
Location C	15687951	15687951	✓	
Location D	17498785	17498795		✓

6. For each item below, select Match or Error based on the location information.

	Original ID	Computer ID	Match?	Error?
Location A	95162348	95162348	✓	
Location B	48159260	48159260	✓	
Location C	75389614	75386914		✓
Location D	14275886	14275386		✓

7. For each item below, select Match or Error based on the location information.

	Original ID	Computer ID	Match?	Error?
Location A	95162348	95163248		✓
Location B	86453132	86453132	✓	
Location C	98746515	98746515	✓	
Location D	86535487	86533487		✓

8. For each item below, select Match or Error based on the location information.

	Original ID	Computer ID	Match?	Error?
Location A	68786432	68786432	✓	
Location B	65487516	65487516	✓	
Location C	98732158	98782158		✓
Location D	65481315	65482315		✓

9. For each item below, select Match or Error based on the location information.

	Original ID	Computer ID	Match?	Error?
Location A	68745612	68745612	✓	
Location B	98735128	98735128	✓	
Location C	32579813	32579813	✓	
Location D	86572354	86542354		✓

10. For each item below, select Match or Error based on the location information.

	Original ID	Computer ID	Match?	Error?
Location A	36925814	36925814	✓	
Location B	74108523	74105823		✓
Location C	91370546	91370536		✓
Location D	82469510	82469510	✓	

11. For each item below, select Match or Error based on the location information.

	Original ID	Computer ID	Match?	Error?
Location A	82095135	82059135		✓
Location B	15902675	15902675	✓	
Location C	02583694	02588694		✓
Location D	98795102	98795102	✓	

12. For each item below, select Match or Error based on the location information.

	Original ID	Computer ID	Match?	Error?
Location A	97643150	97643150	✓	
Location B	04258931	04258931	✓	
Location C	84269573	84269573	✓	
Location D	71935820	71983520		✓

13. For each item below, select Match or Error based on the location information.

	Original ID	Computer ID	Match?	Error?
Location A	79426830	79429830		✓
Location B	46560348	46560348	✓	
Location C	58372538	58372538	✓	
Location D	26142805	26141805		✓

14. For each item below, select Match or Error based on the location information.

	Original ID	Computer ID	Match?	Error?
Location A	49439479	49437479		✓
Location B	11592838	11582838		✓
Location C	19176661	19177661		✓
Location D	15409077	15409077	✓	

15. For each item below, select Match or Error based on the location information.

	Original ID	Computer ID	Match?	Error?
Location A	43456966	43456966	✓	
Location B	46506376	46504376		✓
Location C	33268253	33268253	✓	
Location D	64215069	64215169		✓

16. For each item below, select Match or Error based on the location information.

	Original ID	Computer ID	Match?	Error?
Location A	88652128	88653128		✓
Location B	56610418	56610418	✓	
Location C	57870420	57870420	✓	
Location D	69209826	69209826	✓	

17. For each item below, select Match or Error based on the location information.

	Original ID	Computer ID	Match?	Error?
Location A	72444684	72444684	✓	
Location B	95773686	95793686		✓
Location C	76378875	76368875		✓
Location D	72135969	72136969		✓

18. For each item below, select Match or Error based on the location information.

	Original ID	Computer ID	Match?	Error?
Location A	90900156	90900156	✓	
Location B	68900552	68930552		✓
Location C	72094913	72094913	✓	
Location D	51271014	51274014		✓

19. For each item below, select Match or Error based on the location information.

	Original ID	Computer ID	Match?	Error?
Location A	26982457	26982457	✓	
Location B	94095062	94025062		✓
Location C	63272990	63272990	✓	
Location D	44295107	44297107		✓

20. For each item below, select Match or Error based on the location information.

	Original ID	Computer ID	Match?	Error?
Location A	82128839	82129839		✓
Location B	68289006	68289006	✓	
Location C	52907596	52907596	✓	
Location D	28227723	28227723	✓	

21. For each item below, select Match or Error based on the location information.

	Original ID	Computer ID	Match?	Error?
Location A	68567100	68566100		✓
Location B	73862981	73862781		✓
Location C	67846118	67846118	✓	
Location D	16946105	16943105		✓

22. For each item below, select Match or Error based on the location information.

	Original ID	Computer ID	Match?	Error?
Location A	72498563	72498563	✓	
Location B	39263392	39263392	✓	
Location C	69523174	69523174	✓	
Location D	99774702	99774602		✓

23. For each item below, select Match or Error based on the location information.

	Original ID	Computer ID	Match?	Error?
Location A	93923101	93923101	✓	
Location B	40817887	40817887	✓	
Location C	22224719	22224519		✓
Location D	76408391	76488391		✓

24. For each item below, select Match or Error based on the location information.

	Original ID	Computer ID	Match?	Error?
Location A	58931018	58931318		✓
Location B	21687895	21687895	✓	
Location C	81617552	81607552		✓
Location D	72662730	72660730		✓

25. **For each item below, select Match or Error based on the location information.**

	Original ID	Computer ID	Match?	Error?
Location A	60817689	60817689	✓	
Location B	74810718	74810718	✓	
Location C	71289593	71289493		✓
Location D	19303877	19403877		✓

26. **For each item below, select Match or Error based on the location information.**

	Original ID	Computer ID	Match?	Error?
Location A	87291287	87291287	✓	
Location B	88171963	88171963	✓	
Location C	14336481	14336781		✓
Location D	33667181	33667381		✓

27. **For each item below, select Match or Error based on the location information.**

	Original ID	Computer ID	Match?	Error?
Location A	54740008	54740008	✓	
Location B	20521722	20531722		✓
Location C	65652342	65632342		✓
Location D	85717802	85717802	✓	

28. **For each item below, select Match or Error based on the location information.**

	Original ID	Computer ID	Match?	Error?
Location A	28632485	28632285		✓
Location B	19859026	19859026	✓	
Location C	58403102	58401102		✓
Location D	39443515	39443715		✓

29. **For each item below, select Match or Error based on the location information.**

	Original ID	Computer ID	Match?	Error?
Location A	78238763	78238763	✓	
Location B	91022709	91002709		✓
Location C	55733072	55723072		✓
Location D	57295524	57295524	✓	

30. **For each item below, select Match or Error based on the location information.**

	Original ID	Computer ID	Match?	Error?
Location A	30549609	30559609		✓
Location B	34446110	34446110	✓	
Location C	54662685	54665685		✓
Location D	47912729	47912729	✓	

31. For each item below, select Match or Error based on the location information.

	Original ID	Computer ID	Match?	Error?
Location A	58331778	58321778		✓
Location B	55189381	55159381		✓
Location C	81644273	81634273		✓
Location D	75605336	75603336		✓

32. For each item below, select Match or Error based on the location information.

	Original ID	Computer ID	Match?	Error?
Location A	80408384	80408284		✓
Location B	61260887	61260787		✓
Location C	28797509	28799509		✓
Location D	51416300	51516300		✓

33. For each item below, select Match or Error based on the location information.

	Original ID	Computer ID	Match?	Error?
Location A	53109373	53109373	✓	
Location B	32143083	32142083		✓
Location C	91223224	91223224	✓	
Location D	14552776	14552776	✓	

34. For each item below, select Match or Error based on the location information.

	Original ID	Computer ID	Match?	Error?
Location A	11809006	11829006		✓
Location B	15568587	15568587	✓	
Location C	82160507	82160507	✓	
Location D	53454595	53454595	✓	

35. For each item below, select Match or Error based on the location information.

	Original ID	Computer ID	Match?	Error?
Location A	34467731	34497731		✓
Location B	11171247	11181247		✓
Location C	79770614	79790614		✓
Location D	20367640	20367640	✓	

36. For each item below, select Match or Error based on the location information.

	Original ID	Computer ID	Match?	Error?
Location A	97562674	97562674	✓	
Location B	32604914	32624914		✓
Location C	62193067	62193067	✓	
Location D	99088502	99098502		✓

37. For each item below, select Match or Error based on the location information.

	Original ID	Computer ID	Match?	Error?
Location A	12311507	12311507	✓	
Location B	36729898	36749898		✓
Location C	70719704	70729704		✓
Location D	13693222	13692222		✓

38. For each item below, select Match or Error based on the location information.

	Original ID	Computer ID	Match?	Error?
Location A	49022344	49022344	✓	
Location B	80569455	80569455	✓	
Location C	22832563	22832563	✓	
Location D	32762781	32762681		✓

39. For each item below, select Match or Error based on the location information.

	Original ID	Computer ID	Match?	Error?
Location A	38196223	38196223	✓	
Location B	17818696	17818796		✓
Location C	29683817	29683717		✓
Location D	93146096	93145096		✓

40. For each item below, select Match or Error based on the location information.

	Original ID	Computer ID	Match?	Error?
Location A	77239168	77229168		✓
Location B	42328437	42338437		✓
Location C	49125799	49125799	✓	
Location D	53109485	53109485	✓	

41. For each item below, select Match or Error based on the location information.

	Original ID	Computer ID	Match?	Error?
Location A	27753362	27783362		✓
Location B	59506846	59506846	✓	
Location C	67398900	67388900		✓
Location D	29121080	29141080		✓

42. For each item below, select Match or Error based on the location information.

	Original ID	Computer ID	Match?	Error?
Location A	49033789	49035789		✓
Location B	46429221	46429421		✓
Location C	26877631	26879631		✓
Location D	28324624	28224624		✓

43. For each item below, select Match or Error based on the location information.

	Original ID	Computer ID	Match?	Error?
Location A	43015356	43015356	✓	
Location B	85773680	85773680	✓	
Location C	50993771	50993971		✓
Location D	45812892	45812892	✓	

44. For each item below, select Match or Error based on the location information.

	Original ID	Computer ID	Match?	Error?
Location A	88073391	88072391		✓
Location B	83784310	83784310	✓	
Location C	44343369	44343369	✓	
Location D	21680327	21680227		✓

45. For each item below, select Match or Error based on the location information.

	Original ID	Computer ID	Match?	Error?
Location A	11684811	11686811		✓
Location B	96964470	96964170		✓
Location C	64054952	64053952		✓
Location D	48300787	48300787	✓	

46. For each item below, select Match or Error based on the location information.

	Original ID	Computer ID	Match?	Error?
Location A	14392821	14392021		✓
Location B	78672967	78672967	✓	
Location C	23157271	23158271		✓
Location D	67024446	67024446	✓	

47. For each item below, select Match or Error based on the location information.

	Original ID	Computer ID	Match?	Error?
Location A	96981284	96981284	✓	
Location B	70992418	70992418	✓	
Location C	10638963	10628963		✓
Location D	19094600	19094600	✓	

48. For each item below, select Match or Error based on the location information.

	Original ID	Computer ID	Match?	Error?
Location A	32136298	32166298		✓
Location B	45553898	45553898	✓	
Location C	16633354	16633354	✓	
Location D	15390014	15300014		✓

Work Your Register

1.

Transaction Total: $3.77 Amount Paid: $20.00 Change Due: $16.23			
0	1	1	1
$20	$10	$5	$1
0	2	0	3
$0.25	$0.10	$0.05	$0.01

2.

Transaction Total: $34.10 Amount Paid: $100.00 Change Due: $65.90			
3	0	1	0
$20	$10	$5	$1
3	1	1	0
$0.25	$0.10	$0.05	$0.01

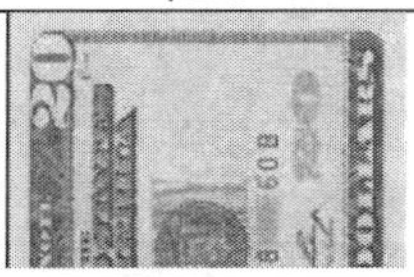

3.

Transaction Total: $6.80 Amount Paid: $10.00 Change Due: $3.20			
0	0	0	3
$20	$10	$5	$1
0	2	0	0
$0.25	$0.10	$0.05	$0.01

4.

Transaction Total: $8.72 Amount Paid: $20.00 Change Due: $11.28			
0	1	0	1
$20	$10	$5	$1
1	0	0	3
$0.25	$0.10	$0.05	$0.01

5.

Transaction Total: $53.17 Amount Paid: $60.00 Change Due: $6.83			
0	0	1	1
$20	$10	$5	$1
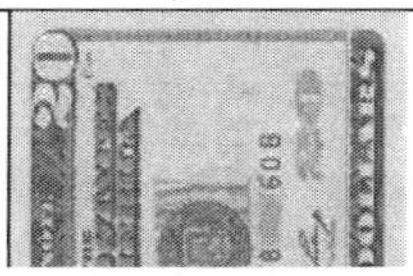			
3	0	1	3
$0.25	$0.10	$0.05	$0.01

6.

Transaction Total: $9.10 Amount Paid: $10.00 Change Due: $0.90			
0	0	0	0
$20	$10	$5	$1
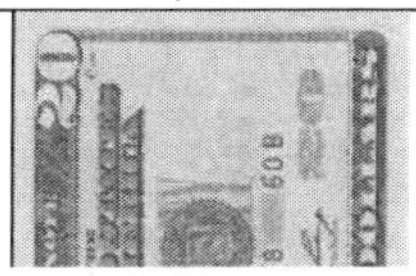			
3	1	1	0
$0.25	$0.10	$0.05	$0.01

7.

Transaction Total: $3.48 Amount Paid: $5.00 Change Due: $1.52			
0	0	0	1
$20	$10	$5	$1
2	0	0	2
$0.25	$0.10	$0.05	$0.01

8.

Transaction Total: $9.23 Amount Paid: $10.00 Change Due: $0.77			
0	0	0	0
$20	$10	$5	$1
3	0	0	2
$0.25	$0.10	$0.05	$0.01

9.

Transaction Total: $70.13
Amount Paid: $100.00
Change Due: $29.87

1	0	1	4
$20	$10	$5	$1
3	1	0	2
$0.25	$0.10	$0.05	$0.01

10.

Transaction Total: $12.09
Amount Paid: $20.00
Change Due: $7.91

0	0	1	2
$20	$10	$5	$1
3	1	1	1
$0.25	$0.10	$0.05	$0.01

11.

Transaction Total: $43.08 Amount Paid: $50.00 Change Due: $6.92			
0	0	1	1
$20	$10	$5	$1
3	1	1	2
$0.25	$0.10	$0.05	$0.01

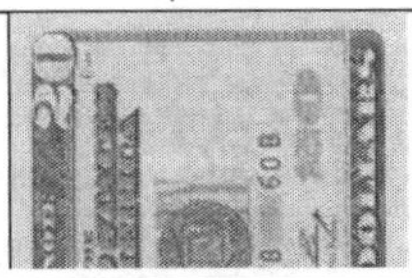

12.

Transaction Total: $1.29 Amount Paid: $10.00 Change Due: $8.71			
0	0	1	3
$20	$10	$5	$1
2	2	0	1
$0.25	$0.10	$0.05	$0.01

13.

Transaction Total: $20.67 Amount Paid: $30.00 Change Due: $9.33			
0	0	1	4
$20	$10	$5	$1
		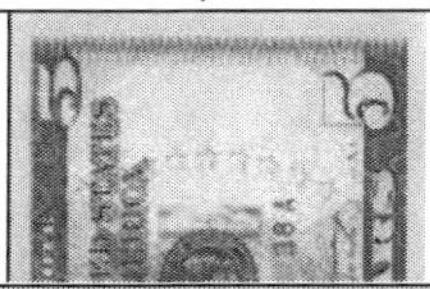	
1	0	1	3
$0.25	$0.10	$0.05	$0.01

14.

Transaction Total: $47.72 Amount Paid: $60.00 Change Due: $12.28			
0	1	0	2
$20	$10	$5	$1
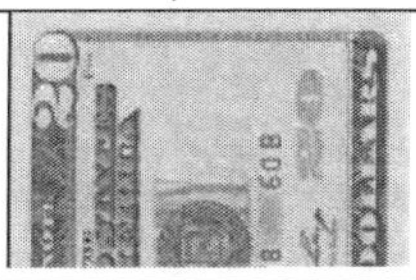			
1	0	0	3
$0.25	$0.10	$0.05	$0.01

15.

Transaction Total: $25.48 Amount Paid: $26.00 Change Due: $0.52			
0	0	0	0
$20	$10	$5	$1
2	0	0	2
$0.25	$0.10	$0.05	$0.01

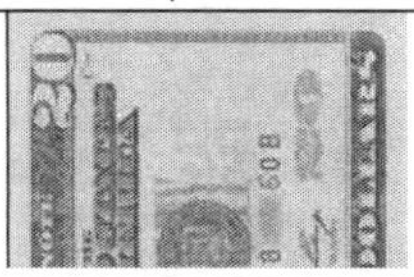

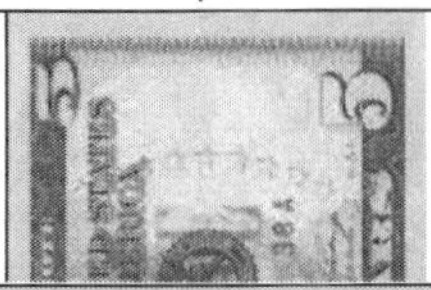

16.

Transaction Total: $14.24 Amount Paid: $20.00 Change Due: $5.76			
0	0	1	0
$20	$10	$5	$1
3	0	0	1
$0.25	$0.10	$0.05	$0.01

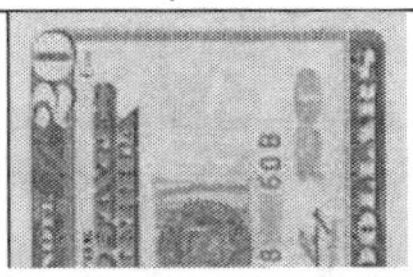

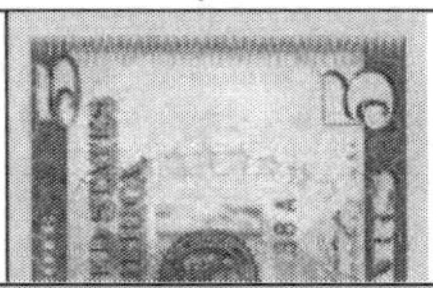

17.

Transaction Total: $52.46 Amount Paid: $70.00 Change Due: $17.54			
0	1	1	2
$20	$10	$5	$1
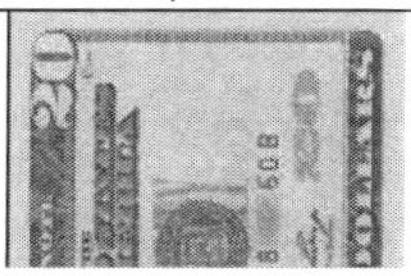			
2	0	0	4
$0.25	$0.10	$0.05	$0.01

18.

Transaction Total: $51.13 Amount Paid: $55.00 Change Due: $3.87			
0	0	0	3
$20	$10	$5	$1

3	1	0	2
$0.25	$0.10	$0.05	$0.01

19.

Transaction Total: $4.18 Amount Paid: $10.00 Change Due: $5.82			
0	0	1	0
$20	$10	$5	$1
3	0	1	2
$0.25	$0.10	$0.05	$0.01

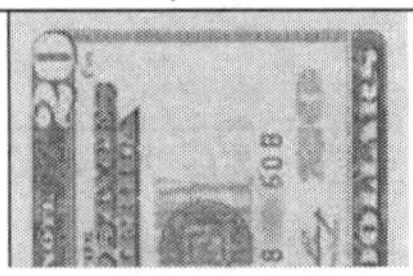

20.

Transaction Total: $54.41 Amount Paid: $60.00 Change Due: $5.59			
0	0	1	0
$20	$10	$5	$1
2	0	1	4
$0.25	$0.10	$0.05	$0.01

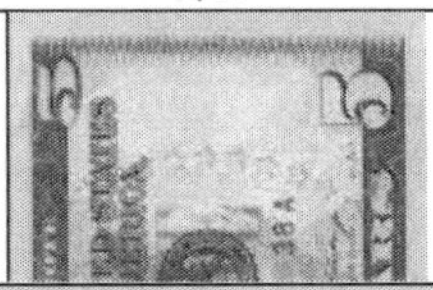

21.

Transaction Total: $79.62 Amount Paid: $80.00 Change Due: $0.38			
0	0	0	0
$20	$10	$5	$1

1	1	0	3
$0.25	$0.10	$0.05	$0.01

22.

Transaction Total: $86.86 Amount Paid: $100.00 Change Due: $13.14			
0	1	0	3
$20	$10	$5	$1
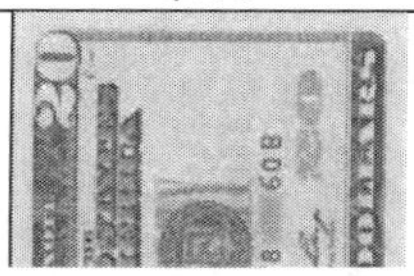			
0	1	0	4
$0.25	$0.10	$0.05	$0.01

23.

Transaction Total: $70.94 Amount Paid: $80.00 Change Due: $9.06			
0	0	1	4
$20	$10	$5	$1
0	0	1	1
$0.25	$0.10	$0.05	$0.01

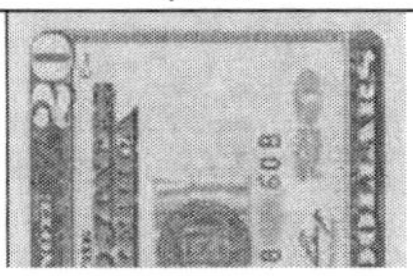

24.

Transaction Total: $21.60 Amount Paid: $50.00 Change Due: $28.40			
1	0	1	3
$20	$10	$5	$1
1	1	1	0
$0.25	$0.10	$0.05	$0.01

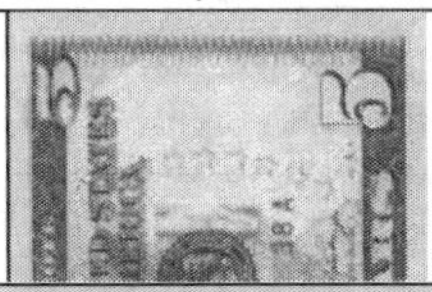

25.

Transaction Total: $3.04 Amount Paid: $5.00 Change Due: $1.96			
0	0	0	1
$20	$10	$5	$1
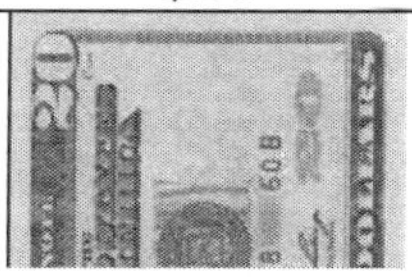			
3	2	0	1
$0.25	$0.10	$0.05	$0.01

26.

Transaction Total: $76.98 Amount Paid: $100.00 Change Due: $23.02			
1	0	0	3
$20	$10	$5	$1

0	0	0	2
$0.25	$0.10	$0.05	$0.01

27.

Transaction Total: $51.78 Amount Paid: $52.00 Change Due: $0.22			
0	0	0	0
$20	$10	$5	$1
0	2	0	2
$0.25	$0.10	$0.05	$0.01

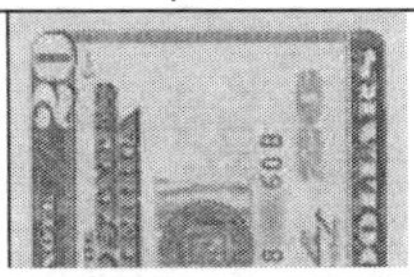

28.

Transaction Total: $45.13 Amount Paid: $60.00 Change Due: $14.87			
0	1	0	4
$20	$10	$5	$1
3	1	0	2
$0.25	$0.10	$0.05	$0.01

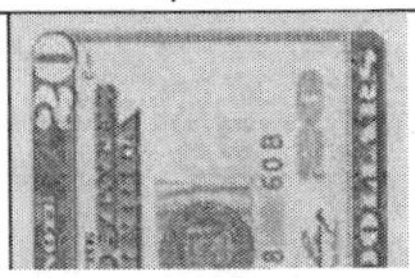

29.

Transaction Total: $30.32
Amount Paid: $40.00
Change Due: $9.68

0	0	1	4
$20	$10	$5	$1
2	1	1	3
$0.25	$0.10	$0.05	$0.01

30.

Transaction Total: $44.04
Amount Paid: $100.00
Change Due: $55.96

2	1	1	0
$20	$10	$5	$1
3	2	0	1
$0.25	$0.10	$0.05	$0.01

31.

Transaction Total: $68.77 Amount Paid: $80.00 Change Due: $11.23			
0	1	0	1
$20	$10	$5	$1

0	2	0	3
$0.25	$0.10	$0.05	$0.01

32.

Transaction Total: $33.02 Amount Paid: $50.00 Change Due: $16.98			
0	1	1	1
$20	$10	$5	$1
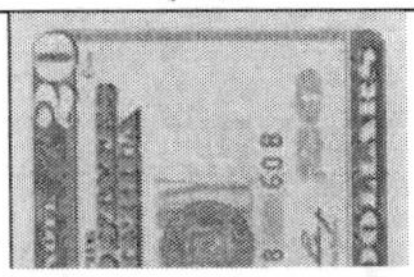			
3	2	0	3
$0.25	$0.10	$0.05	$0.01

33.

Transaction Total: $26.56 Amount Paid: $30.00 Change Due: $3.44			
0	0	0	3
$20	$10	$5	$1
1	1	1	4
$0.25	$0.10	$0.05	$0.01

34.

Transaction Total: $76.72 Amount Paid: $100.00 Change Due: $23.28			
1	0	0	3
$20	$10	$5	$1
1	0	0	3
$0.25	$0.10	$0.05	$0.01

35.

Transaction Total: $2.83
Amount Paid: $5.00
Change Due: $2.17

0	0	0	2
$20	$10	$5	$1
0	1	1	2
$0.25	$0.10	$0.05	$0.01

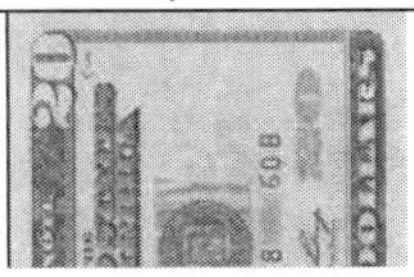

36.

Transaction Total: $77.83
Amount Paid: $90.00
Change Due: $12.17

0	1	0	2
$20	$10	$5	$1
0	1	1	2
$0.25	$0.10	$0.05	$0.01

37.

Transaction Total: $25.61 Amount Paid: $40.00 Change Due: $14.39			
0	1	0	4
$20	$10	$5	$1
1	1	0	4
$0.25	$0.10	$0.05	$0.01

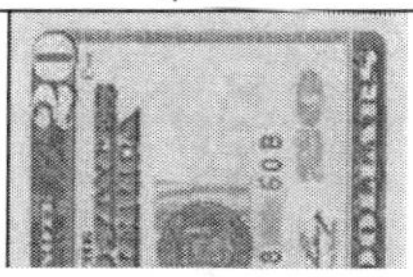

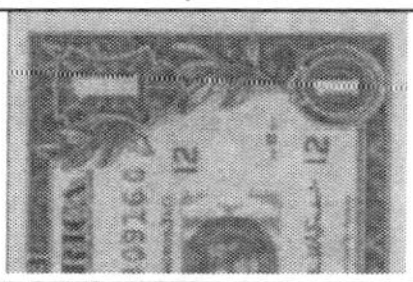

38.

Transaction Total: $17.42 Amount Paid: $20.00 Change Due: $2.58			
0	0	0	2
$20	$10	$5	$1
2	0	1	3
$0.25	$0.10	$0.05	$0.01

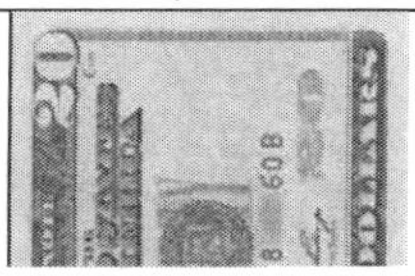

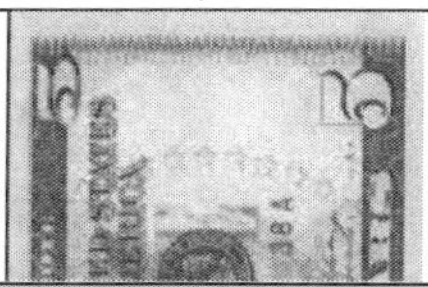

39.

Transaction Total: $47.58 Amount Paid: $50.00 Change Due: $2.42			
0	0	0	2
$20	$10	$5	$1
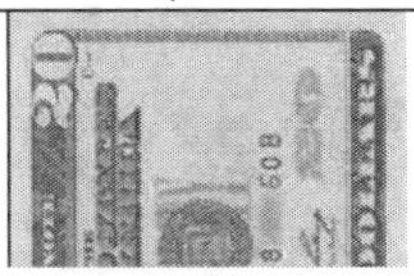			
1	1	1	2
$0.25	$0.10	$0.05	$0.01

40.

Transaction Total: $61.88 Amount Paid: $80.00 Change Due: $18.12			
0	1	1	3
$20	$10	$5	$1
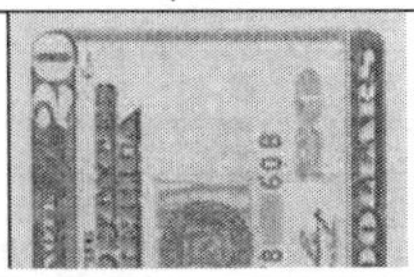			
0	1	0	2
$0.25	$0.10	$0.05	$0.01

41.

Transaction Total: $5.95 Amount Paid: $20.00 Change Due: $14.05			
0	1	0	4
$20	$10	$5	$1
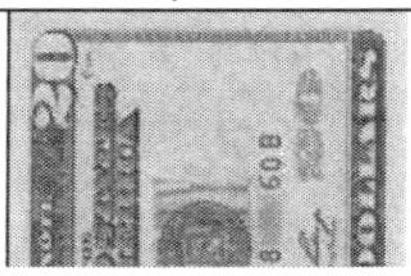			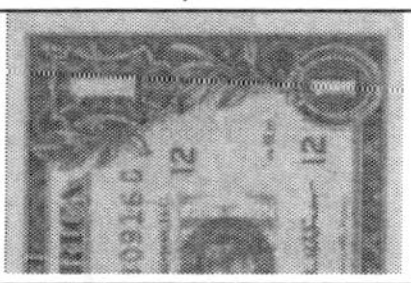
0	0	1	0
$0.25	$0.10	$0.05	$0.01

42.

Transaction Total: $49.92 Amount Paid: $50.00 Change Due: $0.08			
0	0	0	0
$20	$10	$5	$1
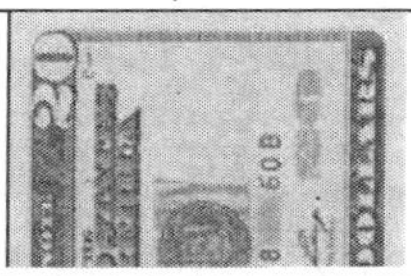			
0	0	1	3
$0.25	$0.10	$0.05	$0.01

43.

Transaction Total: $25.76 Amount Paid: $30.00 Change Due: $4.24			
0	0	0	4
$20	$10	$5	$1
0	2	0	4
$0.25	$0.10	$0.05	$0.01

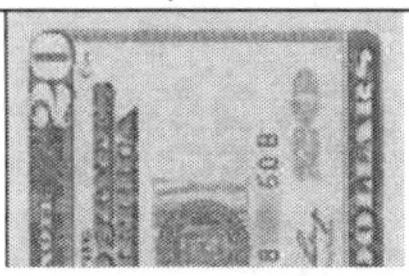

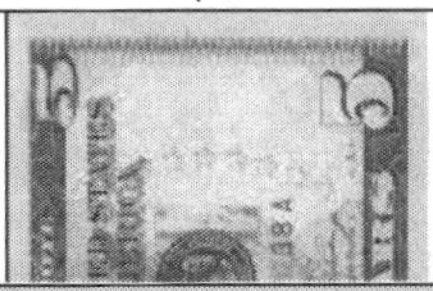

44.

Transaction Total: $7.94 Amount Paid: $50.00 Change Due: $42.06			
2	0	0	2
$20	$10	$5	$1
0	0	1	1
$0.25	$0.10	$0.05	$0.01

45.

Transaction Total: $82.24 Amount Paid: $85.00 Change Due: $2.76			
0	0	0	2
$20	$10	$5	$1
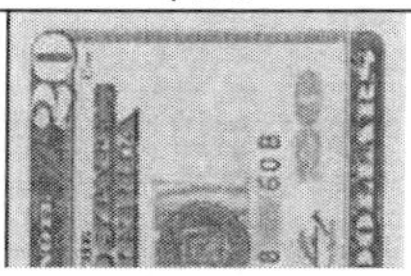			
3	0	0	1
$0.25	$0.10	$0.05	$0.01

46.

Transaction Total: $90.84 Amount Paid: $100.00 Change Due: $9.16			
0	0	1	4
$20	$10	$5	$1
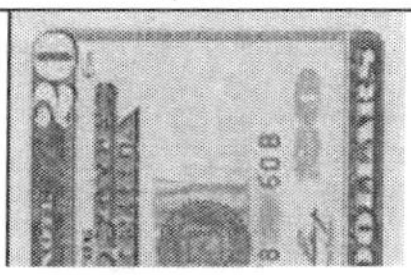			
0	1	1	1
$0.25	$0.10	$0.05	$0.01

47.

Transaction Total: $54.12 Amount Paid: $60.00 Change Due: $5.88			
0	0	1	0
$20	$10	$5	$1
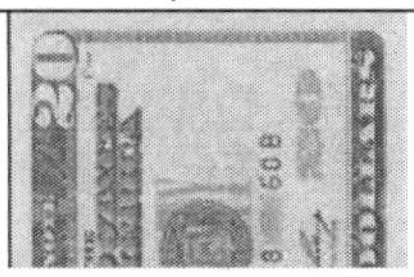			
3	1	0	3
$0.25	$0.10	$0.05	$0.01

48.

Transaction Total: $63.14 Amount Paid: $100.00 Change Due: $36.86			
1	1	1	1
$20	$10	$5	$1
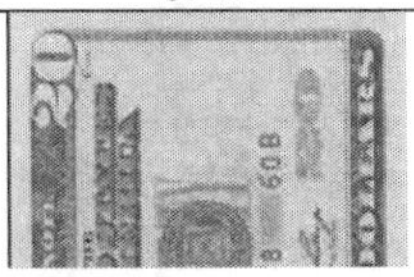			
3	1	0	1
$0.25	$0.10	$0.05	$0.01

How to Overcome Test Anxiety

Just the thought of taking a test is enough to make most people a little nervous. A test is an important event that can have a long-term impact on your future, so it's important to take it seriously and it's natural to feel anxious about performing well. But just because anxiety is normal, that doesn't mean that it's helpful in test taking, or that you should simply accept it as part of your life. Anxiety can have a variety of effects. These effects can be mild, like making you feel slightly nervous, or severe, like blocking your ability to focus or remember even a simple detail.

If you experience test anxiety—whether severe or mild—it's important to know how to beat it. To discover this, first you need to understand what causes test anxiety.

Causes of Test Anxiety

While we often think of anxiety as an uncontrollable emotional state, it can actually be caused by simple, practical things. One of the most common causes of test anxiety is that a person does not feel adequately prepared for their test. This feeling can be the result of many different issues such as poor study habits or lack of organization, but the most common culprit is time management. Starting to study too late, failing to organize your study time to cover all of the material, or being distracted while you study will mean that you're not well prepared for the test. This may lead to cramming the night before, which will cause you to be physically and mentally exhausted for the test. Poor time management also contributes to feelings of stress, fear, and hopelessness as you realize you are not well prepared but don't know what to do about it.

Other times, test anxiety is not related to your preparation for the test but comes from unresolved fear. This may be a past failure on a test, or poor performance on tests in general. It may come from comparing yourself to others who seem to be performing better or from the stress of living up to expectations. Anxiety may be driven by fears of the future—how failure on this test would affect your educational and career goals. These fears are often completely irrational, but they can still negatively impact your test performance.

Elements of Test Anxiety

As mentioned earlier, test anxiety is considered to be an emotional state, but it has physical and mental components as well. Sometimes you may not even realize that you are suffering from test anxiety until you notice the physical symptoms. These can include trembling hands, rapid heartbeat, sweating, nausea, and tense muscles. Extreme anxiety may lead to fainting or vomiting. Obviously, any of these symptoms can have a negative impact on testing. It is important to recognize them as soon as they begin to occur so that you can address the problem before it damages your performance.

The mental components of test anxiety include trouble focusing and inability to remember learned information. During a test, your mind is on high alert, which can help you recall information and stay focused for an extended period of time. However, anxiety interferes with your mind's natural processes, causing you to blank out, even on the questions you know well. The strain of testing during anxiety makes it difficult to stay focused, especially on a test that may take several hours. Extreme anxiety can take a huge mental toll, making it difficult not only to recall test information but even to understand the test questions or pull your thoughts together.

Effects of Test Anxiety

Test anxiety is like a disease—if left untreated, it will get progressively worse. Anxiety leads to poor performance, and this reinforces the feelings of fear and failure, which in turn lead to poor performances on subsequent tests. It can grow from a mild nervousness to a crippling condition. If allowed to progress, test anxiety can have a big impact on your schooling, and consequently on your future.

Test anxiety can spread to other parts of your life. Anxiety on tests can become anxiety in any stressful situation, and blanking on a test can turn into panicking in a job situation. But fortunately, you don't have to let anxiety rule your testing and determine your grades. There are a number of relatively simple steps you can take to move past anxiety and function normally on a test and in the rest of life.

Physical Steps for Beating Test Anxiety

While test anxiety is a serious problem, the good news is that it can be overcome. It doesn't have to control your ability to think and remember information. While it may take time, you can begin taking steps today to beat anxiety.

Just as your first hint that you may be struggling with anxiety comes from the physical symptoms, the first step to treating it is also physical. Rest is crucial for having a clear, strong mind. If you are tired, it is much easier to give in to anxiety. But if you establish good sleep habits, your body and mind will be ready to perform optimally, without the strain of exhaustion. Additionally, sleeping well helps you to retain information better, so you're more likely to recall the answers when you see the test questions.

Getting good sleep means more than going to bed on time. It's important to allow your brain time to relax. Take study breaks from time to time so it doesn't get overworked, and don't study right before bed. Take time to rest your mind before trying to rest your body, or you may find it difficult to fall asleep.

Along with sleep, other aspects of physical health are important in preparing for a test. Good nutrition is vital for good brain function. Sugary foods and drinks may give a burst of energy but this burst is followed by a crash, both physically and emotionally. Instead, fuel your body with protein and vitamin-rich foods.

Also, drink plenty of water. Dehydration can lead to headaches and exhaustion, especially if your brain is already under stress from the rigors of the test. Particularly if your test is a long one, drink water during the breaks. And if possible, take an energy-boosting snack to eat between sections.

Along with sleep and diet, a third important part of physical health is exercise. Maintaining a steady workout schedule is helpful, but even taking 5-minute study breaks to walk can help get your blood pumping faster and clear your head. Exercise also releases endorphins, which contribute to a positive feeling and can help combat test anxiety.

When you nurture your physical health, you are also contributing to your mental health. If your body is healthy, your mind is much more likely to be healthy as well. So take time to rest, nourish your body with healthy food and water, and get moving as much as possible. Taking these physical steps will make you stronger and more able to take the mental steps necessary to overcome test anxiety.

Mental Steps for Beating Test Anxiety

Working on the mental side of test anxiety can be more challenging, but as with the physical side, there are clear steps you can take to overcome it. As mentioned earlier, test anxiety often stems from lack of preparation, so the obvious solution is to prepare for the test. Effective studying may be the most important weapon you have for beating test anxiety, but you can and should employ several other mental tools to combat fear.

First, boost your confidence by reminding yourself of past success—tests or projects that you aced. If you're putting as much effort into preparing for this test as you did for those, there's no reason you should expect to fail here. Work hard to prepare; then trust your preparation.

Second, surround yourself with encouraging people. It can be helpful to find a study group, but be sure that the people you're around will encourage a positive attitude. If you spend time with others who are anxious or cynical, this will only contribute to your own anxiety. Look for others who are motivated to study hard from a desire to succeed, not from a fear of failure.

Third, reward yourself. A test is physically and mentally tiring, even without anxiety, and it can be helpful to have something to look forward to. Plan an activity following the test, regardless of the outcome, such as going to a movie or getting ice cream.

When you are taking the test, if you find yourself beginning to feel anxious, remind yourself that you know the material. Visualize successfully completing the test. Then take a few deep, relaxing breaths and return to it. Work through the questions carefully but with confidence, knowing that you are capable of succeeding.

Developing a healthy mental approach to test taking will also aid in other areas of life. Test anxiety affects more than just the actual test—it can be damaging to your mental health and even contribute to depression. It's important to beat test anxiety before it becomes a problem for more than testing.

Study Strategy

Being prepared for the test is necessary to combat anxiety, but what does being prepared look like? You may study for hours on end and still not feel prepared. What you need is a strategy for test prep. The next few pages outline our recommended steps to help you plan out and conquer the challenge of preparation.

Step 1: Scope Out the Test

Learn everything you can about the format (multiple choice, essay, etc.) and what will be on the test. Gather any study materials, course outlines, or sample exams that may be available. Not only will this help you to prepare, but knowing what to expect can help to alleviate test anxiety.

Step 2: Map Out the Material

Look through the textbook or study guide and make note of how many chapters or sections it has. Then divide these over the time you have. For example, if a book has 15 chapters and you have five days to study, you need to cover three chapters each day. Even better, if you have the time, leave an extra day at the end for overall review after you have gone through the material in depth.

If time is limited, you may need to prioritize the material. Look through it and make note of which sections you think you already have a good grasp on, and which need review. While you are studying, skim quickly through the familiar sections and take more time on the challenging parts. Write out your plan so you don't get lost as you go. Having a written plan also helps you feel more in control of the study, so anxiety is less likely to arise from feeling overwhelmed at the amount to cover.

Step 3: Gather Your Tools

Decide what study method works best for you. Do you prefer to highlight in the book as you study and then go back over the highlighted portions? Or do you type out notes of the important information? Or is it helpful to make flashcards that you can carry with you? Assemble the pens, index cards, highlighters, post-it notes, and any other materials you may need so you won't be distracted by getting up to find things while you study.

If you're having a hard time retaining the information or organizing your notes, experiment with different methods. For example, try color-coding by subject with colored pens, highlighters, or post-it notes. If you learn better by hearing, try recording yourself reading your notes so you can listen while in the car, working out, or simply sitting at your desk. Ask a friend to quiz you from your flashcards, or try teaching someone the material to solidify it in your mind.

Step 4: Create Your Environment

It's important to avoid distractions while you study. This includes both the obvious distractions like visitors and the subtle distractions like an uncomfortable chair (or a too-comfortable couch that makes you want to fall asleep). Set up the best study environment possible: good lighting and a comfortable work area. If background music helps you focus, you may want to turn it on, but otherwise keep the room quiet. If you are using a computer to take notes, be sure you don't have any other windows open, especially applications like social media, games, or anything else that could distract you. Silence your phone and turn off notifications. Be sure to keep water close by so you stay hydrated while you study (but avoid unhealthy drinks and snacks).

Also, take into account the best time of day to study. Are you freshest first thing in the morning? Try to set aside some time then to work through the material. Is your mind clearer in the afternoon or evening? Schedule your study session then. Another method is to study at the same time of day that you will take the test, so that your brain gets used to working on the material at that time and will be ready to focus at test time.

Step 5: Study!

Once you have done all the study preparation, it's time to settle into the actual studying. Sit down, take a few moments to settle your mind so you can focus, and begin to follow your study plan. Don't give in to distractions or let yourself procrastinate. This is your time to prepare so you'll be ready to fearlessly approach the test. Make the most of the time and stay focused.

Of course, you don't want to burn out. If you study too long you may find that you're not retaining the information very well. Take regular study breaks. For example, taking five minutes out of every hour to walk briskly, breathing deeply and swinging your arms, can help your mind stay fresh.

As you get to the end of each chapter or section, it's a good idea to do a quick review. Remind yourself of what you learned and work on any difficult parts. When you feel that you've mastered the material, move on to the next part. At the end of your study session, briefly skim through your notes again.

But while review is helpful, cramming last minute is NOT. If at all possible, work ahead so that you won't need to fit all your study into the last day. Cramming overloads your brain with more information than it can process and retain, and your tired mind may struggle to recall even previously learned information when it is overwhelmed with last-minute study. Also, the urgent nature of cramming and the stress placed on your brain contribute to anxiety. You'll be more likely to go to the test feeling unprepared and having trouble thinking clearly.

So don't cram, and don't stay up late before the test, even just to review your notes at a leisurely pace. Your brain needs rest more than it needs to go over the information again. In fact, plan to finish your studies by noon or early afternoon the day before the test. Give your brain the rest of the day to relax or focus on other things, and get a good night's sleep. Then you will be fresh for the test and better able to recall what you've studied.

Step 6: Take a Practice Test

Many courses offer sample tests, either online or in the study materials. This is an excellent resource to check whether you have mastered the material, as well as to prepare for the test format and environment.

Check the test format ahead of time: the number of questions, the type (multiple choice, free response, etc.), and the time limit. Then create a plan for working through them. For example, if you have 30 minutes to take a 60-question test, your limit is 30 seconds per question. Spend less time on the questions you know well so that you can take more time on the difficult ones.

If you have time to take several practice tests, take the first one open book, with no time limit. Work through the questions at your own pace and make sure you fully understand them. Gradually work up to taking a test under test conditions: sit at a desk with all study materials put away and set a timer. Pace yourself to make sure you finish the test with time to spare and go back to check your answers if you have time.

After each test, check your answers. On the questions you missed, be sure you understand why you missed them. Did you misread the question (tests can use tricky wording)? Did you forget the information? Or was it something you hadn't learned? Go back and study any shaky areas that the practice tests reveal.

Taking these tests not only helps with your grade, but also aids in combating test anxiety. If you're already used to the test conditions, you're less likely to worry about it, and working through tests until you're scoring well gives you a confidence boost. Go through the practice tests until you feel comfortable, and then you can go into the test knowing that you're ready for it.

Test Tips

On test day, you should be confident, knowing that you've prepared well and are ready to answer the questions. But aside from preparation, there are several test day strategies you can employ to maximize your performance.

First, as stated before, get a good night's sleep the night before the test (and for several nights before that, if possible). Go into the test with a fresh, alert mind rather than staying up late to study.

Try not to change too much about your normal routine on the day of the test. It's important to eat a nutritious breakfast, but if you normally don't eat breakfast at all, consider eating just a protein bar. If you're a coffee drinker, go ahead and have your normal coffee. Just make sure you time it so that the caffeine doesn't wear off right in the middle of your test. Avoid sugary beverages, and drink enough water to stay hydrated but not so much that you need a restroom break 10 minutes into the test. If your test isn't first thing in the morning, consider going for a walk or doing a light workout before the test to get your blood flowing.

Allow yourself enough time to get ready, and leave for the test with plenty of time to spare so you won't have the anxiety of scrambling to arrive in time. Another reason to be early is to select a good seat. It's helpful to sit away from doors and windows, which can be distracting. Find a good seat, get out your supplies, and settle your mind before the test begins.

When the test begins, start by going over the instructions carefully, even if you already know what to expect. Make sure you avoid any careless mistakes by following the directions.

Then begin working through the questions, pacing yourself as you've practiced. If you're not sure on an answer, don't spend too much time on it, and don't let it shake your confidence. Either skip it and come back later, or eliminate as many wrong answers as possible and guess among the remaining ones. Don't dwell on these questions as you continue—put them out of your mind and focus on what lies ahead.

Be sure to read all of the answer choices, even if you're sure the first one is the right answer. Sometimes you'll find a better one if you keep reading. But don't second-guess yourself if you do immediately know the answer. Your gut instinct is usually right. Don't let test anxiety rob you of the information you know.

If you have time at the end of the test (and if the test format allows), go back and review your answers. Be cautious about changing any, since your first instinct tends to be correct, but make sure you didn't misread any of the questions or accidentally mark the wrong answer choice. Look over any you skipped and make an educated guess.

At the end, leave the test feeling confident. You've done your best, so don't waste time worrying about your performance or wishing you could change anything. Instead, celebrate the successful completion of this test. And finally, use this test to learn how to deal with anxiety even better next time.

Review Video: Test Anxiety
Visit mometrix.com/academy and enter code: 100340

Important Qualification

Not all anxiety is created equal. If your test anxiety is causing major issues in your life beyond the classroom or testing center, or if you are experiencing troubling physical symptoms related to your anxiety, it may be a sign of a serious physiological or psychological condition. If this sounds like your situation, we strongly encourage you to seek professional help.

Additional Bonus Material

Due to our efforts to try to keep this book to a manageable length, we've created a link that will give you access to all of your additional bonus material:

mometrix.com/bonus948/postalvea